DISCARD

THE AMERICAN HOME

TRADITIONAL STYLE FOR TODAY

THE AMERICAN HOME

TRADITIONAL STYLE FOR TODAY

ELLEN M. PLANTE

1035237

Lumpkin

FRIEDMAN/FAIRFAX
PUBLISHERS

GIFT

A FRIEDMAN/FAIRFAX BOOK

© 2000 by Michael Friedman Publishing Group, Inc.

All rights reserved. No part of this publication may be reproduced, stored in a retrieval system, or transmitted, in any form or by any means, electronic, mechanical, photocopying, recording, or otherwise, without prior written permission from the publisher.

ISBN 1-56799-994-8

Editors: Francine Hornberger and Reka Simonsen
Art Director: Jeff Batzli
Designer: Meredith Miller
Photography Editor: Valerie E. Kennedy
Production Manager: Richela Fabian

Color separations by Colourscan Overseas Co. Pte. Ltd.
Printed in Hong Kong by Sing Cheong Printing Company Ltd.

1 3 5 7 9 10 8 6 4 2

For bulk purchases and special sales, please contact:
Friedman/Fairfax Publishers
Attention: Sales Department
15 West 26th Street
New York, NY 10010
212/685-6610   FAX 212/685-1307

Visit our website:
www.metrobooks.com

For those who admire the timeless beauty and elegance of traditional style.

With special thanks to my editors, Francine Hornberger and Reka Simonsen, of the Michael Friedman Publishing Group, Inc.

CONTENTS

INTRODUCTION

Today's traditional home combines classic style with welcome comfort. "Tradition" is of course the key word here—a word that speaks volumes about who we are and how we surround ourselves with the things we love. And perhaps more so than in years gone by, tradition is also something we've come to crave in order to balance hectic, high-tech lives. As a result, the traditional home is more than just a safe haven; it is our personal comfort zone with rooms designed around smart, timeless style. Traditional home design affords us a soothing connection with the past that blends effortlessly with the present.

Whether you aspire to create rooms that speak of formal elegance or relaxed comfort, or something in between, traditional style offers diversity and vitality. Furniture of fine craftsmanship, a sophisticated or playful use of color, an eye for detail, and room settings of beautiful proportions are the very heart and soul of the style. Thus it comes as no surprise that a traditional decorating scheme has constant, broad-range appeal.

For well over two hundred years, North American homes have showcased traditional design interiors. The elegant Queen Anne furnishings of the eighteenth century and the classical nineteenth-century designs of Federal pieces gave rise to interiors associated with striking architectural details. Soon, Victorian furnishings filled rooms to overflowing, and by the end of the nineteenth century the focus shifted to quality handcrafted items, furniture, wallpapers, and accessories that found expression in the form of the Arts and Crafts style.

Today, a traditional decor can incorporate the classical furniture and interior design motifs popular during the first half of the nineteenth century, or a period look can take its cue from a specific time in history. To provide a better appreciation of the almost limitless possibilities associated with a traditional decor, a brief look at the furniture styles and interior designs of days gone by will serve as a fitting introduction to the beautiful, idea-filled photographs in the chapters that follow.

OPPOSITE: This early Federal-style living room is a stunning tribute to neoclassical design. Corinthian columns make dramatic room dividers and add an architectural flair that complements the carved legs of the chairs and sofa. Accents—from the rug with the stylized Greek key border and the gilt-framed mirror to the formal window treatment and candlestick lamp chandeliers—intensify the neoclassical appeal.

ABOVE: This inviting conversation area is proof positive that black and white can be beautiful. Matching upholstered easy chairs are dressed with plump pillows, and an ottoman can do double duty as a coffee table or a place to rest your feet. Yards of soft, billowing fabric have been transformed into a stunning window treatment that complements this classic setting. Note, too, the Staffordshire spaniel that enhances the traditional air.

Traditional Furniture Styles

By the early eighteenth century, homes were increasing in size, and greater attention was given to furnishings and interior details. From 1720 to about 1750, the Queen Anne style (also known as Baroque) took center stage, and these beautifully proportioned furnishings were crafted from native North American woods such as maple and walnut, or from more costly imported mahogany.

At this time, the colonies were very much influenced by styles in England, but as Queen Anne chairs, tables, and chests made their way into Colonial homes, the cabinetmakers and

cabinetmakers were making the journey to the New World to introduce the latest furniture form—the Chippendale style. Word of the new style spread with the 1754 publication of Thomas Chippendale's book of designs, *The Gentlemen and Cabinet Maker's Director*, and the style remained in vogue until the 1790s. This book governed furniture design in both Europe and North America for several decades, and indeed its influence is still felt today. While Chippendale's name is associated with the style, it is also referred to as Rococo, because of the French influence so evident in the decorative scrollwork and carvings on

craftsmen that fashioned these graceful pieces often interpreted the designs differently. While early, formal Queen Anne furnishings were designed and produced in growing urban centers, such as Boston and New York, smaller cabinetmaker shops along the eastern coast were also turning out simpler "country" examples of the popular style.

Common furniture pieces created in the Queen Anne style include drop-leaf dining tables, side chairs, armchairs, tea tables, high chests of drawers, upholstered wing chairs, game tables, and tilt-top tables. The most noteworthy element of this design style is the softly curving lines that define the cabriole leg and the top rail of chair backs. Other hallmarks of the style include shell carvings on case pieces and furniture legs, cabriole legs with padded feet, a vase-form splat on chair backs, and butterfly-style drawer pulls on chests and tables.

Furniture styles and interior design fashions tended to overlap during the eighteenth and nineteenth centuries, so it comes as no surprise that while Queen Anne furnishings were still highly favored in North America, English

many of these period pieces. Sometimes the style is also called Georgian, after the English monarchs that occupied the throne in Great Britain between 1714 and 1820.

Chippendale-style furnishings were not a drastic departure from the Queen Anne style, but the level of ornamentation increased and the soft curves associated with chairs and table legs were replaced with more obvious curvatures. In short, it was a bolder, more masculine look. Walnut, cherry, and imported mahogany were the woods favored for furniture construction, and popular pieces included large chest-on-chest case pieces, tall case clocks, low chests of drawers, upholstered camel-back sofas, bombé chests of drawers, serpentine-front chests of drawers, slant-top desks, high chests with bonnet tops, Pembroke tables (with drop leaves), tea tables, candle stands, corner chairs, side chairs, upholstered open armchairs (also called lolling chairs), easy chairs, and card tables.

Eye-catching details on furniture in the Chippendale style include the top crest rails with ears and scrollwork on chairs, the ball-and-claw foot,

OPPOSITE: Recalling the Colonial past, this elegant dining room features white walls with a mustard-colored chair rail, carved mantel, and cupboard. In keeping with the spirit of the style, furnishings pay tribute to the timeless beauty of Queen Anne design. A large area rug adds bright color and a sense of warmth, while the oil portrait above the hearth and silver candlesticks are fine and fitting touches.

ABOVE: This period-perfect sitting room is furnished with handsome pieces in the Chippendale style, including the lovely upholstered wing chairs, tall case clock, drop-leaf table, and corner chair. Appropriate decorative touches include an Oriental area rug atop the wide plank flooring, porcelain jars and candlesticks on display, and the bayberry-green paint selected for interior trim and window moldings.

a straight bracket foot or ogee bracket foot on case pieces, ornately carved Rococo shells on chests, decorative rosettes and finials on large pieces such as case clocks, and straight legs (often with Oriental fretwork) on chairs, tables, and camel-back sofas.

The classical designs associated with ancient Greece and Rome inspired the next style of furniture and architecture, which was popular from the 1790s to the early 1800s. Early neoclassical style (known in the United States as Federal style) evolved as a direct result of several factors, including the archaeological discoveries in Italy at Pompeii and Herculaneum. The War of Independence brought major changes to North America, and architectural designs, interior decorations, and urnishings took on a crisper, lighter look.

Cabinetmakers who crafted neoclassical furniture were influenced by design books that were published by such familiar names as George Hepplewhite, Thomas Sheraton, and Duncan Phyfe, who was highly regarded for his work in this style. Hallmarks of the Federal style include the use of classical motifs, veneer, and ornamentation such as inlay (decorative work formed by setting contrasting woods into the surface of a piece).

The cabriole leg of earlier Queen Anne and Chippendale furniture disappeared, and chairs and tables now sported thin, straight legs. Rather than the curved crest rails on chair backs, Federal or early neoclassical pieces had a more rectangular look. Chair splats included vase and urn shapes as well as a shield-back design that was popular on chairs with a more oval shape.

Common furniture pieces produced in the Federal style included drop-leaf side tables, desks with a tambour front, ladies' worktables, settees, serpentine-front sideboards, combination desk/bookcases, and oval dining tables. Classical ornamentation included fluting and inlaid bellflower, eagle, and fan motifs; swag and tassel festoons; and gilt trim or decorations. Federal pieces proved highly popular, not only for their clean look but for the extraordinary beauty that resulted from the contrast of light and dark woods used in inlays. While cabinetmakers in coastal cities and such urban centers as Philadelphia excelled at this particular style, rural country craftsmen and

⟨⟩

OPPOSITE: A neoclassical chair and table with obvious Sheraton styling (note the square chair back) are positioned against a backdrop featuring a leaf-and-vine motif. The appealing wallpaper is accented with a framed botanical print and a bouquet of white roses. A sculpture made from a violin gives the classical decor a personal touch.
ABOVE: Casual country style makes for a warm and inviting dining room. A pine farm table and black Windsor chairs sit before a beautiful hearth of aged wood. A second table is placed between the unadorned windows to act as a handy buffet or a home for country treasures. Wide plank flooring and the period paint color used for the trim add an authentic touch. Accessories, such as the pewter chandelier and daffodils, reinforce the country theme.

members of the Shaker community developed their own simplified but striking take on the Federal style.

Shaker furnishings are especially suitable in a country-inspired period setting. The Shaker sect (a religious group) strived for simplicity, purity, order, and harmony in their daily lives as well as in their surroundings. The first Shaker community was founded near Albany, New York, in 1776, and soon other communities were founded in Connecticut, Massachusetts, New Hampshire, Maine, Ohio, Kentucky, and Indiana. The Shaker settlement at Mount Lebanon, New York, was by far the largest.

The Shaker cabinetmakers used such native woods as pine, maple, chestnut, birch, cherry, and butternut for their simple furnishings. Devoid of all

ABOVE: Colonial roots blend with the beautiful simplicity of Shaker style in this charming dining room.
A large tavern table is outfitted with Windsor arm chairs and Shaker-inspired ladder-back chairs with
woven seats, while a collection of baskets and crockery becomes a focal point in the background.

LEFT: Taking its decorative cue from the Victorian era, this traditional parlor boasts an eye-catching wallpaper border, an ornately carved overmantel, and furnishings befitting the period theme. Twin settees in elegant upholstery are joined by a marble-topped Renaissance Revival–style table that's perfect for refreshments and a bouquet of fresh flowers. Period light fixtures, a decorative fire screen, and the collection of family portraits convey the spirit of Victoriana.

furnishings until 1930. As popular today as they were two hundred years ago, Shaker furnishings are truly an example of classic, enduring design.

The second wave of neoclassical furniture design, known as Empire style, debuted around 1815 and remained popular until the late 1840s. A pronounced French influence mingled with the classic ornamentations associated with ancient Greece and Rome, and the result was furniture with a heavier, more masculine look than that of earlier neoclassical pieces.

ornamentation, their long tables, benches, cupboards, and chairs were constructed with exposed dovetail joints and sturdy wooden pegs used as drawer pulls. Their early chairs had splint, cane, or leather seats, while examples from the late 1800s included rush or colorful tape seats.

Utilitarian Shaker furnishings may have had an obvious lack of ornamentation and decorative hardware, but the style was impressive nonetheless because of its simple beauty, its quality workmanship, and the joyful colors (red, green, blue, and yellow) used in painted finishes. Shaker chairs, benches, and rockers were even sold to the public through catalogs, and the furniture became quite popular after a display at the 1876 Philadelphia Centennial Exhibition won an award.

Shaker communities continued to attract followers through the 1860s, but after that their numbers began to decline. Only several hundred members remained after 1900, but they continued to produce a limited amount of

Ornamentation became more obvious and in some cases more elaborate, with marble inlays and detailed carvings. Mahogany, satinwood, and rosewood were often used to craft Empire furnishings, but such native woods as cherry and maple were put to use as well and stained to imitate their more costly cousins.

The introduction of the Empire style brought new furniture forms into the home, most notably the center table, which became a permanent fixture in the drawing room or parlor for several decades to come. Other popular pieces included the French-inspired sleigh bed, the Grecian sofa (actually a reclining sofa), and the substantial-looking pier table.

Empire-style chairs with lyre backs or cane seats were commonly used in the dining room, and massive dining tables often had paw feet with casters.

Various pieces of furniture were decorated with gilt or stenciled classical designs, brass tacks, elaborate water-leaf or bald eagle carvings, inlay decorations, cut glass or pressed glass knobs, and gilding to imitate the gilt bronze mountings on the most costly examples of Empire-style pieces.

As with the styles previously mentioned, major cities continued to be important centers of furniture design and production. Duncan Phyfe, for example, who was widely recognized for his craftsmanship in both the Federal and Empire styles, had a shop in New York City until the mid-1840s. Cabinetmaking began to change, however, with the introduction of the circular saw. Production costs were reduced and furniture could be turned out much more quickly, thus satisfying the demand of the growing middle class for fashionable, well-furnished homes.

By 1840 the neoclassical designs that had reigned supreme for fifty years or so gave way to a series of Victorian revival styles that conveyed romanticism and eclecticism. Three furnishing styles were predominant from 1840 to 1880: Gothic Revival, Rococo Revival, and Renaissance Revival. Of these three, the Rococo Revival style is perhaps the purest and most beautiful embodiment of nineteenth-century romanticism.

Victorian Rococo Revival–style furnishings were inspired by the furniture designs popular in France during the 1700s. Crafted mainly of black walnut and rosewood, these fanciful pieces had delicate, curvaceous shapes with serpentine curves, cabriole legs, and carved ornamentations in the shapes of flowers, fruit, birds, scrolls, and tendrils. Many upholstered pieces were covered with horsehair, but the more expensive furnishings turned out by cabinetmakers were covered with beautiful brocades or damasks.

Rococo Revival–style tables often featured marble tops, and with the Industrial Revolution well under way, furniture manufacturers were able to sell matching suites to outfit the Victorian parlor. The balloon-back chair

⟨≡×≡⟩

ABOVE: This Empire-style settee is upholstered with forest green velvet and given a whimsical touch with green and white checkered pillows, proving that a beautiful furniture form is always appealing. A gilt-framed portrait hangs in the background, and the classic decor is enhanced by an Oriental rug.

OPPOSITE: The timeless beauty of traditional style conveys a warm welcome in this elegant entryway. Cream-colored walls provide the perfect backdrop for handsome hardwood flooring and a beautiful center table—a venerable Empire-style design with roots in the early nineteenth century. Gilt light fixtures, a striking floral arrangement, and a notable convex mirror add to the formal appeal.

⬦※⬦

OPPOSITE: Fine, handcrafted furniture and an emphasis on natural materials and motifs are the hallmarks of the Arts and Crafts style. This classic interior features warm oak in both the architecture and the furnishings, and art glass is used for the cabinet doors and the hanging lamp. Even the throw pillows on the rockers convey a strong sense of period style, thanks to their stylized floral designs.

was used in the dining room as well as the parlor, and the ornate étagère (an elaborate piece of furniture with open shelves to display bric-a-brac) was a product of the Rococo Revival style.

Machine-made furnishings were produced for middle-class homes, but the wealthy purchased handcrafted furniture made by such firms as Joseph Meeks and Sons or master cabinetmaker John Henry Belter. During the 1850s, Belter opened a factory in New York City, and his work achieved such a level of beauty and success that his name became synonymous with the style. His furniture was especially popular among well-to-do Southerners, many of whom commissioned his firm to outfit their plantation homes.

The highly embellished (and sometimes inferior) mass-produced furnishings of the Victorian age came under the close scrutiny of social reformers, first in Great Britain and Europe and then in North America. By the 1860s, Englishman William Morris had founded a company that not only produced wallpapers and textiles, but also hand-built oak furnishings that were inspired by the medieval period. The work of Morris' firm did not go unnoticed, and before long others were joining the growing reform movement that called for quality handcrafted furnishings in simple, honest designs. While several such reform groups developed in England, the founding of the Arts and Crafts Exhibition Society in 1888 gave a name to the new style. Thereafter, a full-fledged movement was under way to encourage the harmonious blending of creativity, artistic endeavors, and fine craftsmanship in furnishings and decorative accessories.

The Arts and Crafts movement in North America developed around 1890, after both Elbert Hubbard and Gustav Stickley had journeyed to England and seen firsthand the products of the movement there. Hubbard returned home and established the Roycroft Community in East Aurora, New York, where a group of artisans produced simple oak furnishings as well as books, metalwork pieces, and lighting fixtures for the home. Stickley operated a furniture factory near Syracuse, New York, where he, too, produced simplified, linear oak furniture associated with the new reform style.

Two of his brothers went on to establish the L. & J.G. Stickley Company, which also turned out Arts and Crafts–inspired furnishings.

Today the furniture of the Arts and Crafts movement is also referred to as Mission style, and while most of the quality pieces were handcrafted from quartersawn oak, maple was also used. Chairs, tables, and settees were designed for the living and dining rooms, and bedroom furnishings as well as desks and rockers were popular items. Upholstered pieces were usually covered in leather or canvas, and brass, copper, or iron hardware or fittings turned up on case pieces. Pegged joints are a signature of the style.

The popularity of Arts and Crafts– or Mission-style furnishings began to decline around 1915 because of the inferior quality of some of the mass-produced, machine-made pieces that were turned out by imitators who tried to offer the latest style at the lowest price. Also, the outbreak of World War I shifted the world's attention and new styles followed, such as Art Deco, which was the darling of the modernistic movement in furniture and interior design between 1918 and 1940.

Traditional Interior Design

North American interest in architectural and interior design styles began with the Colonial period, which spanned the years from 1720 until the 1780s. Timber-framed, saltbox, brick, stone, and fashionable Georgian homes of English design were the most common styles of housing during the eighteenth century. Depending upon the size of the house and the family's income, interiors during the early Colonial period often had plaster walls and ceilings, perhaps baseboard moldings and cornices, window moldings, and chair rails. In the larger homes of the wealthy, paneling was a popular wall treatment until the mid-eighteenth century.

Plaster walls were painted in bright colors, such as primrose yellow, robin's-egg blue, red, or forest green, and trim work was often painted as well. Those walls that were not painted during the late Colonial era may have been wallpapered or treated to a fabric covering such as watered silk. Popular wallpapers imported from France had scenic designs or were flocked in imitation of such luxurious fabrics as velvet.

The fireplace, always a focal point in the home, took on a more formal tone during the Colonial era with the addition of a handsome mantel. In upper-class homes, imported marble was used, and in smaller homes, the mantel was often painted to look like marble. Overmantels were also popular and often featured paneling or architectural embellishments, such as broken pediments, Doric pilasters, or period engravings.

Most floors in the Colonial home were constructed of pine planking and covered with decorative floorcloths and hand-loomed or rag rugs. In the finest homes, expensive wool Oriental or Aubusson rugs (tapestrylike rugs imported from France) were used.

Window treatments during the Colonial era included curtains and draperies to frame and cover the six-over-six, nine-over-nine, or twelve-over-twelve glass windowpanes. Velvet, printed cotton, and brocatelle were the fabrics of choice for draperies in the homes of the gentry, and these window treatments were often accessorized with a decorative cornice. It was during this period that arched Palladian windows made their debut in elegant Georgian-style homes.

Furnishings during the early Colonial period were in the Queen Anne style, followed by the introduction of the Chippendale design. In addition, many homes featured ornately detailed built-in wall or corner cabinets to store and display the family's precious silver, china, and crystal. Along with these cherished items, other decorative accessories in the Colonial home may have included wood-framed mirrors, wall-hung tapestries, family portraits, oil paintings, and silver or brass candlesticks or candelabra.

After the American Revolution came to a close in 1783, new homes were constructed in the Federal style that were based on pattern books originally published in England and promoted by a growing number of professional architects. These elegant homes and town houses were inspired by neoclassical designs and remained popular from the 1790s through the 1830s. The Federal-style home proved to be the perfect backdrop for the first wave of popular classic furnishings.

Interior architectural features included delicate columns that framed doorways, and beautiful elliptical fanlights, sidelights, or decorative carvings and moldings. Classical motifs such as swags, festoons, and urns were carved into cornices and ceiling medallions. Built-in china cabinets with glazed doors were featured in dining rooms, and ornate bookcases with diamond-patterned glazed doors were often incorporated into the parlor or elegant drawing room. Neoclassical designs were also featured on fireplace surrounds via carvings or applied composition detailing.

Wall treatments in the Federal-style home included French wallpapers with scenic vistas or patterns of subtle stripes, combinations of stripes and

OPPOSITE: The massive hearth is the focal point of this cozy sitting area. Such design elements as the deep red paneled wall and warm pine flooring clearly recall the Colonial past. The spirit of the period is cheerfully conveyed in the crazy quilt and matching pillow on the sofa, the Windsor chairs pulled close to the fire, and the vintage trunk used as a casual coffee table. A traditional decor need not be formal to impart a strong sense of style.

stars, or classical motifs. Painted plaster walls in colors such as white, rose, or medium green sometimes included a wooden wainscot with a chair rail. With the emphasis on light and airy interiors, woodwork around doors and windows was frequently painted white.

Floors were made of pine boards that were painted or stenciled. Floor coverings included straw matting, canvas floorcloths, or more costly Oriental, Aubusson, or English Wilton rugs. In an upper-class home, the entryway might have featured a marble floor.

Neoclassical Federal-style furnishings were upholstered with rich fabrics, such as satin, taffeta, damask, or velvet. Chintz was also used, as was toile de Jouy, a French cotton fabric featuring single-color pictorial scenes on a white background. Furnishings were arranged symmetrically within the room, and pairs of matching sofas and chairs were popular for a very elegant look.

Windows during the Federal period were covered with draperies made of brocatelle, silk, taffeta, voile, muslin, or velvet. Common patterns included stripes and floral graphics. In keeping with the neoclassical theme, fabric festoons appeared at drapery tops, or carved wooden cornices served as a decorative cap.

The second wave of neoclassical design brought about the Greek Revival period that began in the 1820s and lasted through the 1850s. Homes in the Greek Revival style were either quite grand, with impressive columned porticos, or of a simpler design, with off-center front doors featuring a rectangular transom light and narrow sidelights. Rural homes or farmhouses, covered in clapboard or constructed of brick, used corner boards or plasters and stone lintels to help give the impression of a Greek temple.

The simplicity of the Greek Revival interior was the ideal setting for the Empire-style furnishings that outfitted the homes of the period. Interior architectural embellishments included door moldings and fireplace surrounds with carved Greek key designs and thin, columned pilasters. The eagle and the anthemion or honeysuckle design were other common motifs in carvings and plasterwork.

❦

OPPOSITE: Symmetry and harmony are often hallmarks of traditional design. Here, a coffee table vignette is created to reflect balance.
The hearth is dressed with a beautiful mantel that showcases a gilt-trimmed portrait and matching sconces of petite candlestick lamps.
ABOVE: Elegant Chippendale-style furnishings take center stage in this well-appointed dining room. The table is surrounded with chairs
sporting the signature cabriole (curved) leg with ornamental feet. White upholstered seat cushions blend effortlessly with the room's
neutral backdrop. For a splash of color and period flair, the windows have been dressed with cranberry-red draperies that
make a decidedly formal statement.

⫸❈⫷

OPPOSITE: A modern interpretation of the Colonial canopy bed becomes the focal point in this young girl's bedroom. Thanks to the combination of soft colors, beautiful patterns, and textures that vary from the white wicker chairs to the sheer bed curtains, this traditional bedroom will be stylish and lovely for years to come.

Plaster walls in the Greek Revival–style home were painted white, a soft pastel, gray, or terra-cotta, and woodwork was painted white. If a wallpaper was used in the drawing room, it typically featured neoclassical designs, such as acanthus leaves or rosettes, or geometric patterns. Wainscoting was no longer used, but substantial baseboards, plasterwork, ceiling medallions, and floor-length windows with shutters added notable architectural interest.

While homes of the well-to-do had been featuring costly carpets in the best rooms, during this early-nineteenth-century period it was customary to purchase room-size rugs with neoclassical or floral motifs. They proved a beautiful decorative element in combination with plain painted walls and the more masculine sofas, tables, and desks designed in the Empire style. These furnishings were lined up around the room in a symmetrical fashion, both for practical reasons and for formal flair.

Upholstery on Empire furnishings was of rich fabrics with stripes or patriotic themes, and window dressings often included a muslin undercurtain with draperies tied back to create a swag effect. Shutters were also used on windows, as were painted shades. Window hardware or drapery poles were decorative, and sometimes a handsome fabric was simply draped across the pole side-swag fashion. Fringe and beautiful fabric borders became popular embellishments on simple fabrics used for window treatments. Among the decorative accessories used in the home during the neoclassical period were gilt-framed mirrors, wall sconces and candelabra used for lighting, porcelain, fine china, and brass objects.

Romanticism took center stage by the year 1840, and until around 1900 several architectural designs, furniture styles, and popular modes of interior decoration that are categorically referred to as Victorian appeared (and overlapped).

Starting with the medieval-inspired Gothic Revival–style houses of the 1840s and Italianate town houses and homes of the 1850s and 1860s, residential buildings became increasingly eclectic, culminating in the beautiful Queen Anne– and Colonial Revival–style homes of the late nineteenth century. Architectural embellishment was a hallmark of these and others styles of the era. A notable example is the Victorian home, which was distinguished by its ornamental "gingerbread" trim, mansard-style roofs, decorative shingles, turrets, bold colors, ornate porches, art glass windows, and often elaborate carpentry work.

The interior of the Victorian home was an architectural treasure trove that evolved from a setting in which white, pastels, and neutral colors were used to one in which muted or somber colors and wallpapers reigned supreme. By the 1870s, the tripartite wall treatment—walls divided into three horizontal areas designated the dado, field, and frieze—was all the rage, and ceilings were often embellished with wallpaper or for a coffered effect. Social reformers were recommending a return to a simpler wall treatment by the 1890s, and the lavish combinations of paint, paper, and paneling gave way once again to either painted or papered walls.

Choices for floor coverings and treatments expanded during the Victorian age to include tile, which was popular in the entryway; parquet flooring; a broad range of decorative, ingrain rugs and Brussels carpets; and linoleum, which was favored for the kitchen during the last quarter of the century.

Furnishings in the various Victorian styles were intimately grouped in a semiformal or informal arrangement around a center table or near the hearth, to allow people to converse comfortably. Upholstered pieces in damask, brocade, or velvet were tufted, tasseled, and braided. Floral prints, such as chintz, were popular for upholstered furnishings, as were deep colors such as dark red.

The Victorian era also was the first to use outdoor spaces as extended living areas. Initially, gardens and porches were furnished with ornate iron chairs and settees as well as more rustic, wooden pieces. Then, by the late nineteenth century, wicker furniture proved ideal for relaxing sunrooms, conservatories, and the roomy front porches found on so many Victorian-era homes. These furniture types shall be explored in greater detail in the chapter devoted to outdoor spaces.

Window treatments during the Victorian age became very elaborate, often incorporating several "layers" of dressings while draperies puddled at the floor. Lace was used as an undercurtain, and fringe, tassels, ornate cornices, and swags made windows yet another focal point in rooms that were already full of decorations.

The Victorian interior also served as a display case for an abundance of decorative accessories. Rooms overflowed with throw pillows, kerosene lamps, gas chandeliers, footstools, fringed shawls draped over tabletops, bric-a-brac, flowers and greenery, artwork and prints, books, and pottery. Compared to the rather stately interiors of the neoclassical period, the Victorian home was a visual wonder.

Change, of course, was inevitable. The Arts and Crafts movement that had begun in England during the late 1800s had a definite impact on North American architecture and interior design by the year 1900. Modest homes referred to as "bungalows" were constructed across the country, but were especially popular in the West. These shingled houses had low-pitched gabled roofs and usually included verandas, and windows were often decorated with leaded glass designs. Bungalows were usually one story and had open floor plans. While simpler interpretations of the style were built in small towns and villages, the main objectives were always craftsmanship, simplicity, and the use of natural elements.

The interiors of the early-twentieth-century Arts and Crafts homes often included beautiful built-in bookcases or cabinets and rustic stone fireplaces or hearths with plain oak mantels. Furnishings during this period were Mission style and conveyed the simplicity, harmony, and durability that were the hallmarks of the style. The backdrop for these sturdy oak pieces included walls painted in soft, muted colors (often earth tones) or wallpapers featuring stylized floral or nature motifs, such as those designed by William Morris. Wooden floors were left bare or accessorized with handsome wool rugs with botanical designs.

The practice of using multilayered window dressings was discarded in favor of simple curtains made of muslin, lace, linen, cotton, cretonne, or linen taffeta. A valance was often used in tandem with window-length curtains looped back to one side. Stenciled borders on curtains or a delicate fabric border enhanced their delicate charm.

Decorative accessories in the Arts and Crafts setting included a careful selection of hand-thrown, hand-decorated pottery, copper metalware (such as lamps with a copper base and an art glass shade), hand-embroidered linens, and blown glass objects. The handcrafted items of the artisan were preferred over the mass-produced bric-a-brac found in homes just a decade earlier. Understated beauty could be found in honest craftsmanship and unassuming objects.

Today's Traditional Home

Although this is by no means an exhaustive list of traditional furnishings and modes of interior design, this information serves as an introduction to the handsome, elegant, and timeless styles that are today considered classic. You may have a deep fondness for Oriental furniture with a lacquered finish, or a love for the sleek, modernistic lines of Art Deco pieces. Perhaps you admire the curvaceous decorative elements of the late-nineteenth-century Art Nouveau period. They are all appropriate and fitting in today's traditional home. If the simple ease and casual comfort associated with country decorating is more to your liking, traditional touches can imbue your rooms with an old-world spirit that conveys a hearty welcome and promises comfort and good looks for years to come.

In today's traditional home, the emphasis is on comfort and timeless design. Regardless of whether you prefer a formal, semiformal, or casual style, your home can be an elegant blend of the past and the present. Rich colors, choice fabrics, and carefully chosen accessories can join together with time-honored furnishings to create the home of your dreams.

Along the way, remember that traditional motifs, period or classical furniture, and a room's design elements can easily be mixed or matched. Regardless of whether you opt for antique furnishings or well-crafted reproductions, each piece can become a focal point in a traditional setting. Add the beauty of color, texture, and pattern via walls, upholstery, and draperies, and the end result will be a signature setting of classic design. Above all, allow your rooms to extend comfort and a warm welcome—just as homes did in years gone by.

Guiding you room by room, the pages that follow present an array of inspiring photographs and design ideas for creating your own wonderful interpretation of classic style.

OPPOSITE: The epitome of classical styling, a beautiful, low four-poster bed presides over this gracious bedroom. Reminiscent of a decorative half-canopy, a lovely floral fabric has been gathered and festooned at the head of the bed to create a striking focal point. Pale blue wallpaper, a collection of favorite books, framed portraits, and an elegant chandelier combine to make the bedroom an inviting retreat.

Chapter One

THE ENTRYWAY

The formal entryway has a long and distinguished history that evolved from architectural styles that were popular throughout the eighteenth century. Prior to that time, limited financial means and concern over meeting the most basic needs, such as shelter, led the colonists to construct simple two-room houses devoid of an entry as we know it today.

By the time the Georgian-style home made its debut during the early 1700s, formality had become a hallmark of the new fashions in architectural design. Homes expanded to include four rooms on the ground floor, with a similar configuration of rooms on the second story. The entryway was actually a central hall with openings into rooms on either side and access to the stately center stairway. This hall served as a passageway into the more public rooms of the house and was outfitted with tables and chairs lined up along the wall. In the larger Georgian homes of successful merchants and businessmen, the entryway was dominated by striking architectural detailing. A graceful arched window was often situated above the doorway, and handsome wood paneling contributed an aristocratic air to the entryway.

Later architectural styles (Federal and Greek Revival) followed suit by including a center hall or side entry that featured a striking stairway as well as a passageway through the home. Architectural detailing, such as the fan-shaped window above the front door on Federal-style homes, and classical motifs used on woodwork and cornices made entryways look as beautiful as the best room in the house.

During the Victorian age, the wide assortment of housing styles created variations on the entryway, but this area was crucial to all homes. By the mid-nineteenth century, the entryway had become so important that specialized furnishings were created specifically for this all-important space. Gothic-inspired hall trees made of iron accommodated cloaks, and handsome wooden examples, often with marble embellishments and mirrors, were manufactured in popular furniture styles. Such pieces stood nicely against a backdrop of papered walls and marble, tile, or parquet floors.

⊰⊱

OPPOSITE: Striking architectural details and high-style furnishings create a timeless and elegant foyer. An ornate chandelier, delicate molding, marble flooring, and a high ceiling painted to resemble the sky contribute to the formal feeling.
ABOVE: This entryway is graced with a handsome stairway. Architectural detailing—including a notable cornice, the diamond-patterned floor, and the elegant railing on the staircase—set the tone for patrician furnishings and accessories. An elegant settee upholstered in a classic striped fabric is joined by a gilt plant stand and an umbrella stand that serves to display a collection of walking sticks.

LEFT: This welcoming entryway conveys the classic beauty of a traditional decor by showcasing elegant and handsome, dark, wooden furnishings and accessories. White walls make the foyer appear more spacious, while a simple window treatment admits considerable light. A beautiful vase filled with blooms and a collection of canes add timeless appeal.

personal style and timeless good looks. Period furnishings chosen to suit the size of the space can become a focal point and should be complemented by a striking background of rich or pastel colors, a notable pattern, and a dose of texture. The entire setting is given a polished look with select accessories, such as a favorite piece of artwork, floral arrangements, or an elegant mirror.

Once the open living plan was introduced with the Arts and Crafts bungalow, the entryway disappeared for a short time. In the bungalow, the front door opened directly into a spacious living room. The corridorlike entry or square-shaped foyer had been eliminated in the name of simplified living and straightforward style.

Fast-forward to the present, and with the exception of all but the most modern homes, the majority of houses today have some sort of transitional space between outdoors and in that serves as an entryway or foyer. Decorating this area in a traditional style means combining practicality with classic design to convey a warm welcome and a feeling of comfort. Not only is this where we greet our guests, but it is the designated area for dealing with coats, boots, and packages, and thus should be furnished to meet personal needs. As a preview to your living spaces you want the entry to be inviting; as a necessary space it must also be functional.

No matter whether your home is large or small, and regardless of its architectural design, you can create an appealing entryway that conveys

The practical aspects of decorating the traditional entryway will often be determined by whether you're dealing with a sizable front hall, a narrow passageway, or an entry adjoining your living room. Flooring is of primary importance in a space that's subject to heavy traffic. Such time-honored favorites as marble, slate, granite, or ceramic tile can prove ideal, thanks to their longevity and washable surfaces. Or a hardwood floor might be favored for its warm patina and can be protected and accessorized with a lovely area rug.

Floor Treatments

Personal style, the amount you wish to invest in flooring, and the advantages of the options available will help determine the floor treatment suitable for your entry. Granite and marble are ideal in a formal setting, and while quite expensive, they virtually last forever. Both come in myriad colors and patterns, but marble featuring the classic veining design is undoubtedly the most elegant. Smooth materials such as these, however, can become slippery when wet. Choosing stone with a textured surface can reduce the problem.

To maintain the beauty of a marble or granite floor, it is wise to apply a sealant appropriate to the material for added protection. A marble floor will also benefit from periodic waxing. And while an area rug can certainly enhance the good looks of a rugged stone floor, this type of floor is beautiful in and of itself and has full decorative impact when left to stand alone.

Slate can also be a wonderful choice for flooring in the entryway, and it is less costly than marble or granite. Slate can be adapted to both formal and casual decorating schemes, and the range of muted colors available makes it ideal in a traditional decor. Slate also has the advantage of being slip-resistant, so it's practical for the entryway, and by applying a sealant, it can be protected from stains.

Ceramic tile is another popular alternative when it comes to flooring in the front entry. Available in many colors, sizes, shapes, and patterns, ceramic tiles even come in versions that offer the look of marble or granite. Ceramic tile is reasonably priced, can stand up to hard use, and is easy to keep clean. In the entryway, an unglazed tile with a matte finish is preferable to avoid a slippery surface. The true beauty of ceramic tile lies in the endless possibilities it gives you to create something truly unique. And while ceramic tile will last for years and is virtually maintenance-free, it's a good idea to use a sealant to protect the grout from stains. Grout, too, is available in a wide selection of colors, so there's no need to settle for the standard white.

If not a masonry floor in the traditional entryway, perhaps a handsome hardwood flooring is more to your taste. It can be used to play up a casual or formal mood, or to tone either mood down a bit. Hardwoods such as oak, maple, and walnut can be stained and/or treated with polyurethane for a glossy water-resistant finish that will last for many months. An Oriental rug in rich, deep colors can be a nice finishing touch.

A polished hardwood floor may be perfect in a formal entryway, but a traditional country decor calls for something a bit more casual. A stenciled design, a color stain, or even "washing" to lighten wood tones can contribute to the more relaxed air of a casual entry. Any of these techniques can be accomplished by a skilled artisan or a determined do-it-yourselfer.

For a traditional entryway that takes its cue from the Victorian age, a parquet floor is every bit as period perfect as a hardwood or tile floor. If your home's decor favors the look of the Arts and Crafts period, an oak hardwood floor dressed with an Oriental or William Morris–inspired rug will contribute to the spirit of the style.

ABOVE: The timeless appeal of a weathered wooden door introduces guests to this homey entryway. Wide plank flooring has been stenciled with a leaf design to evoke the spirit of the outdoors, while pale, creamy walls provide a soothing backdrop. The patina of aged wood on the stairway is accented by a special paint technique that highlights the steps. For a subtle and decorative effect, sea shells are used as doorstops to continue the nature-inspired theme.

RIGHT: Half-paneled walls, geometric wallpaper, and an elegant cornice display subtle shades of green, which prove a fitting backdrop for the commanding staircase. Scale and proportion were carefully considered when the polished drop-leaf table and matching upholstered side chairs were selected for this striking traditional entry. A wall of portraits in gilt frames, candlesticks in hurricane lanterns, and even a collection of vintage fire buckets hanging from above add appeal and a signature touch.

Wall Treatments

After you've decided upon the flooring that meets your needs and helps contribute to the look you wish to create, consider the colors and choices of wall treatments available for the front hall. Actually, your decisions here will often be determined by the color scheme throughout the rest of your home, as well as the size of your entry and available lighting.

Light colors have long been a favorite in small spaces or areas that receive little natural light. Pastels, one of the many variations of white, or such neutral colors as beige, gray, or taupe are especially fitting in an entryway and blend easily with a traditional decor. Also, consider painting doorways off the entry the same light color for a unifying effect.

In contrast, a large entryway or center hall, especially one with an abundance of natural lighting, can well afford a more dramatic treatment through the use of a deep color or handsome wood wainscoting that gives your space a formal air. Then you'll want to decide between using paint or wallpaper, or perhaps a combination of both.

Paint has the advantage of being highly affordable and easily changed should you decide on a different color scheme in a few years. Keep in mind that it is always worth investing in a high-quality paint to ensure a superb finish and pleasing results. High-gloss or semigloss paints work well in a dark entry since they reflect light, while a satin or matte finish is better suited to a bright entry or foyer.

Walls can be painted—or they can be decoratively painted. Ragged walls are a nice touch in a traditional decor and create the illusion of soft, floating fabric. A piece of cheesecloth or a towel is used as a blotter to create the "ragged" design. This is a creative process that often takes some experimentation to achieve the desired results.

Stenciling was a common means of creating decorative walls during the Colonial era, and today there are numerous precut stencil designs available for use in a period or classical setting. After a few practice runs on a scrap board, any homeowner can comfortably tackle this type of decorative effect. A stenciled border is ideal in a small entryway where an accent is desired but more decoration would be overwhelming.

Wallpaper can be a wonderful wall treatment in a traditional entryway, provided that you choose a pattern appropriate for the size of the space. A small front hall will benefit from a small print, whereas a large print can make a spacious foyer seem more welcoming. Floral designs, stripes, and

ABOVE: Sunlight streaming through the entryway and a fresh coat of white paint on the woodwork makes for a pleasing front hall. This welcoming space has a coordinated look thanks to the charming wallpaper, which is especially suited for dealing with slants, curves, and cubbyholes. As the perfect finishing touch, a bouquet of fresh flowers awaits visitors.

subtle geometric patterns all enhance a traditional decor and provide the perfect background for handsome period furnishings.

A wallpaper border is also an excellent choice for a subtle, decorative effect. Available in widths ranging from just a few inches to nineteen inches (48cm), a wallpaper border can create a focal point, or it can be used to tie adjoining areas together.

Compared to other areas of the home, the entryway may be somewhat small on space, but it can be big on architectural details. Look at your walls and ceiling, and keep in mind the level of formality you wish to convey. Something as simple as a chair rail molding can speak of elegance, while a striking ceiling medallion and elaborate cornices will impart a more patrician look. Fortunately, today there are several options when it comes to architectural details, including handcrafted plasterwork, wooden moldings available at the local home-building center, and cost-effective polystyrene, which is surprisingly lightweight. Keep in mind the popular motifs used in period rooms of the past: Baroque and Rococo shells, rosettes, acanthus leaves, bellflowers, fruit carvings, swags, scrolls, eagles, the Greek key motif, and columns.

LEFT: A handsome spiral staircase becomes the focal point in this spacious entry. A minimalist approach to decorating allows the warm wood tones in the flooring, trim work, and staircase to shine. A potted fern and an Oriental rug add just the right amount of contrasting color and texture.

OPPOSITE: Empire-style furnishings take up residence in this lovely neoclassical entryway. Handsome wood flooring and a traditional wall treatment combining a wainscot and painted field (large expanse of wall) create a fitting backdrop for elegant furnishings and a gilt mirror. Beautiful objects, such as the porcelain bowl, brass candlesticks, and small silver vase filled with tulips, are the perfect finishing touches.

Lighting

Lighting in a traditional entryway usually includes one or more of the following: a ceiling fixture, a hanging fixture or chandelier, wall sconces, or a table lamp. Once again, the size of your entryway and the amount of natural lighting it receives will guide you toward the best selections for your setting. In a small entryway, a ceiling fixture with an attractive glass shade can be used in tandem with a small table lamp sporting a traditional pleated shade. In contrast, for a well-proportioned foyer, a beautiful hanging fixture suspended from a classic ceiling medallion is truly elegant and appropriate to the larger space. Wall sconces can be artistic and decorative elements as well as effective, practical sources of light, no matter what the dimensions of the space. There are numerous possibilities to consider and a wide selection of sconce styles from which to choose.

RIGHT: Chippendale-style chairs furnish a large center hall resplendent with architectural details. White wooden paneling used on the lower portion of the walls is complemented by rich parquet flooring and a doorway with an elaborate cornice that features a swag motif. Beautiful wall sconces with shaded mini candlestick lamps light the way from the hall into the other rooms.

Furnishings

Furnishings can take center stage in the entryway, regardless of whether you decide on a single neoclassical shield-back chair and a petite side table, or something more substantial, such as a tall case clock or an antique cupboard. Scale and proportion are the key considerations, as are the more practical concerns such as traffic flow, seating for a visitor, a handy place to stash keys and mail, and a spot to hang coats.

If room allows, a Queen Anne wing chair provides a comfortable spot in which to sit a spell, and a handsome drop-leaf table is a handy surface for a lamp or the display of cherished items. In a narrow entry, a delicate settee might prove more practical.

For those who envision a traditional decor rooted in the late nineteenth century, an ornate Victorian hall tree is as functional as it is lovely. A simplified Arts and Crafts entry makes a welcoming statement with a polished oak coatrack that's linear by design and displays the warm patina of aged wood. A bamboo hall tree or coatrack hints at Oriental design and can also convey the eclectic mind-set of the Victorian age. In a small front hall where space is truly at a premium, Shaker pegs pay tribute to simple beauty and functional design.

The possibilities for furnishing your traditional entry are almost limitless, but once you decide what direction to take, you can determine the accent pieces you wish to display. A traditional setting achieves timeless appeal through the use of accessories, such as crystal, brass, porcelain, gilt-framed prints and mirrors, silver, china, tassels, tapestries, and choice artwork. With this

RIGHT: A beautifully proportioned and veneered table plays host to an elegant vignette in this understated entryway. The soft glow of silver—in the lamp, candlestick, salver, and picture frames—complements the dark, polished wood. The neutral tones of the walls and the stair runner make the space feel light and open.

in mind, you may decide to display a collection of fine prints or porcelain jars, or perhaps a single crystal vase filled with beautiful fresh flowers. Add fringe and tassels to a chair cushion; gather silver candlesticks together on a tabletop—whatever you choose to place front and center in the entryway will reflect your interests and express your personal style. Once accessories have been added, you'll have put the finishing touch on your traditional entryway—a welcoming passage into the home that speaks of fine details and classic comfort and style.

BELOW: Popular furniture designs were often modified, blended, or subject to regional interpretations by North American craftsmen during the eighteenth and early nineteenth centuries. Here, a simplified version of a Chippendale tall case clock presides over a warm and inviting entryway.

LEFT: A Chippendale-style chest-on-chest that incorporates a slant-topped desk is a stunning focal point in this classic entry. A chair with distinct neoclassical lines has been added for pleasurable reading, writing letters, or routine paperwork. Accessories, such as the Oriental rug, cherished china on display, and even the decorative tassel on the case piece, reinforce the traditional decorating scheme.

Chapter Two

THE LIVING ROOM

In many ways the living room has come full circle. What started as the all-purpose keeping room in humble households of the pre-industrial era became known as the hall in the two-story, four-room homes built by the gentry during the early 1700s. Many such homes also included a parlor, which was actually a fine bedroom with the most impressive furnishings. This parlor, complete with a bed, was used for entertaining.

By the middle of the eighteenth century, grand homes in the Georgian style included a separate room for formal activities and entertaining guests. The name "parlor" carried over to this best room, and the bed was moved to a sleeping chamber upstairs. An assortment of tables and chairs and perhaps a settee or two now occupied the formal parlor and were arranged symmetrically around the edges of the room. This formal practice of placing furnishings against the wall not only contributed to the stately appearance of the parlor but also created enough space for tables and chairs to be moved to the center of the room for meals in an age before rooms were set aside specifically for dining.

Attention to detail meant that these early parlors often included chair rails (a practical measure with chairs lined up along walls), plaster ceilings, cornice moldings, and a handsome paneled fireplace wall. Windows increased in size, and mirrors became an important addition to the parlor in the eighteenth century for their ability to reflect candlelight. The parlor of the late 1700s had become a status symbol of sorts, with the size of the home conveying a sense of wealth and genteel living. By dedicating a space to refined entertainment, the homeowner implied that there was ample room upstairs for separate living and sleeping quarters.

◆◆◆

OPPOSITE: During the eighteenth and early nineteenth centuries, gilded wallpaper was favored for its reflective properties. The gold in this royal-patterned wallpaper not only reflects subtle hints of light but adds warmth and splendor to the room. Gold is also employed in the frames and the mirrored ceiling medallion, which adds architectural interest.

ABOVE: A pair of upholstered wing chairs dressed in crisp white keeps the coordinated backdrop of matching wallpaper and window treatment from seeming too busy. Traditional style with a tailored look is achieved by carefully selecting colors and patterns with everlasting appeal. The round table is ideal for displaying a collection of silver trophies, and the Oriental rug anchors the living room.

(especially the bungalow) of the twentieth century, the all-purpose living room took center stage. Family life and entertaining were conducted in the same comfortable space—a concept that often holds true today.

Given the parlor's history as a special room for entertaining, how do we transform today's living room into a modern-day space that meets our needs with solid comfort and yet reflects all the beauty of timeless style? Quite simply, this combination can be achieved by calling upon the period and classical furniture styles that have endured through the ages, or those that have more recently emerged (such as Arts and Crafts style) as leaders in quality design. In addition, the colors, fabrics, patterns, and decorative elements that have assumed center stage in homes of the past can be deftly blended into today's traditional decor to create serene or dramatic settings.

During the early to mid-1800s, middle-class homes also began to reflect a certain measure of formality. Older houses were enlarged to allow for a proper parlor, and new homes, based largely on architectural plan books, included a parlor for entertaining regardless of whether the home was a ottage or mansion. Many homes also included a sitting room for family 0...activities, a concept that lasted throughout the Victorian age.

As more and more customs associated with nineteenth-century culture became obsolete, and as new forms of entertainment replaced the extravagant dinners, social teas, and receptions held in the home, reserving a room for formal entertaining lost significance. With the new architectural designs

Perhaps your personal style dictates a living room that is a new rendition of a Colonial parlor, complete with handsome Queen Anne furnishings, stenciled walls, and wide plank pine flooring that hints at a formal country life. Or maybe you prefer clean lines, delicate furnishings, and ancient designs, in which case a neoclassical decorating scheme can can be used to give your living room elegance and a formal mood. And for those who long for cozy, casual comfort, a living room that recalls the Victorian period can be dressed up or down to create either a romantic or a playful mood. The key to traditional decorating is versatility, and styles can be mixed or matched with stunning results.

⟨⟩

OPPOSITE: Casual elegance abounds in this sunny living room. The fireplace wall adds architectural interest with moldings and recessed shelving that features a carved Rococo shell design. Slipcovered furnishings and woven baskets add a pleasing blend of color and texture. In keeping with the informal air, a sisal rug defines the seating area and accents a hardwood floor.

ABOVE: Camel-back sofas, a design with roots in the Chippendale style, are joined here by elegant, dark wooden furnishings that include a beautiful corner cabinet. Instead of an ornate drapery treatment, white shutters are used at the windows to give this traditional living room architectural appeal and a light and airy feeling.

Color

Color has a strong impact in a traditional living room. The colors chosen for walls, carpeting or area rugs, window dressings, and accessories will often be determined by the color or colors in your upholstery. With this in mind, an understanding of basic color theory can make it easier to plan your decorating scheme. Each color falls into one of three categories: primary, secondary, or tertiary. The primary colors are red, blue, and yellow. A secondary color is then created by blending two primary colors, such as mixing blue and yellow to achieve green. A tertiary color is the end result of mixing a primary and a secondary color (for example, combining blue and green to create teal). No wonder today's color options are almost limitless—there is a pale tint or dark shade available for virtually every hue imaginable.

OPPOSITE: Richly colored walls can make a large room appear more inviting and intimate. In this comfortable living room, teal is used for the walls, the chairs, and even the sponge-painted fireplace, with dark red accents providing splashes of brightness and warmth. Upholstered wing chairs offer a welcome spot in front of the hearth to relax and enjoy a favorite book from the nearby shelves. Books are clearly a strong interest of the owner—even the coffee table is made of them.

RIGHT: Dark walls, a roaring fire, and a medley of colors and patterns make this a warm and inviting living room. The handsome leather sofa is softened with floral throw pillows, and the floral theme is continued in the valance and the fresh bouquets. A lovely pine chest serving as a coffee table and sisal matting keep the room from feeling too formal.

Color is also thought of in terms of warm and cool hues. The warm hues (red, yellow, pink, and orange) are stimulating and energetic, while cool hues (blue, purple, gray, and green) are softer on the eyes and more restful. By combining a warm and a cool hue in a traditional decor, a complementary color scheme is created that is ideal for a period room. In contrast, a monochromatic scheme is achieved by implementing various shades of a single color, and might be perfect for a more classical look. A third color scheme, referred to as analogous, calls upon three or more colors, one of which is a primary color, that are closely related on the color wheel. An analogous color scheme might be fitting in a casual setting, but keep in mind that there are no hard-and-fast rules. Since both dark or vivid hues and light, pale colors have long been used in traditional homes, your personal style should guide you in the color choice you make for your living room. Keep in mind that an open living plan will benefit from a color scheme that flows effortlessly from one room to the next. Hints of gold or bronze will add instant elegance, and walls bathed in neutral hues, such as taupe or beige, or dressed in nature's colors are increasingly being featured in today's traditional home with striking results.

LEFT: Basic white can be stunning and simply elegant. This inviting modern interpretation of traditional style combines hardwood flooring with crisp, painted walls for a neutral backdrop. A series of French doors is draped with airy curtains that won't impede the view, and a white area rug defines the seating space. A graceful twisting design is used for the legs of both tables and the pole lamps to tie the room together further.

Ceilings, too, can be painted for subtle or not-so-subtle impact. Light colors help give the illusion of height to a low ceiling, while a darker shade can make a very high ceiling seem less pronounced. In a formal living room with a beautiful chandelier, emphasize the fixture with a notable ceiling medallion— perhaps a rosette pattern.

Wallpaper in an elegant living room should offer a hint of pattern but not dominate the space. A tailored stripe is perfect in a traditional setting, as are large floral motifs, geometric patterns, scenic wallpapers, or Oriental designs. For a more casual room, consider a small floral or geometric pattern. Small and midsize floral designs are also especially fitting in a Victorian-period setting, and the stylized nature motifs of the late nineteenth century go hand in hand with an Arts and Crafts–inspired living room. The fabric for upholstery and/or draperies can often be matched to wallpaper for a dressy, unified look.

Wallpapers today are available prepasted or unpasted (in which case you must mix and apply glue) with various finishes, such as vinyl coating, for easy cleaning. Thanks to the popularity of wallpaper, many hand-printed papers are being reproduced in the same lovely patterns that held proud places in homes long ago. While these may be more costly than the machine-printed papers available today, hand-printed papers are historically accurate and ideal for a period interior.

Wall Treatments

Once you've chosen the color scheme for your traditional living room, walls can be painted, papered, covered with fabric, paneled, or treated to a wainscot. Paint is by far the simplest solution and one that can have a big visual impact. If your living room tends to feel small and intimate, a variation of white, a neutral hue, or a pastel will make it appear larger and airier. In contrast, in a spacious living room, deep colors can make the space more inviting. Woodwork can be painted white for contrast and to call attention to any architectural details.

Special paint techniques such as combing, ragging, sponge painting, or creating a faux marble effect are popular alternatives to plain painted walls in a traditional setting. These methods impart instant old-world charm and add a dramatic element to the room's decor. Seek the services of a professional, or research a particular technique thoroughly and practice before tackling an entire room.

ABOVE: Colonial style reigns supreme in this well-appointed living room. Intricate wooden paneling and a marble fireplace create a formal ambience that's tempered by cheerful red and white checkered easy chairs and a matching ottoman. Symmetry—in the matching pole lamps and wall sconces above the hearth—enhances a classic interior design. Note, too, how the tailored ottoman can function as an impromptu coffee table.

OPPOSITE: Design elements of traditional style are given a fresh twist in this cheerful living room. A coffered ceiling is brightened with wallpaper between white painted beams; simple yellow draperies magically appear more elegant when hanging from a decorative metal rod; and a playful interpretation of the camel-back sofa makes use of different fabric colors on the cushions and ties the piece together with matching braided trim. Signature touches include the heart-back wooden chair and the modern art displayed on the wall.

ABOVE: A casual arrangement of traditional furnishings lends an informal air to this inviting living room. Creamy yellow wallpaper with a subtle pattern, a handsome marble fireplace, French doors dressed with lavish draperies, and a rug layered over sisal matting impart timeless style. An ornate bronze chandelier and a gilt mirror flanked by wall sconces enhance the decor, as does the simple blue and white pitcher filled with flowers.

LEFT: An assortment of colors and patterns makes this living room most inviting. A carved wooden mantel supported by Corinthian columns turns the fireplace into an instant focal point, and the oval mirror is a fitting accent. Plump easy chairs and a floral-print sofa invite curling up in front of the hearth. Fresh flowers, Staffordshire spaniels atop the mantel, and favorite paintings add decorative and highly personal notes.

Similar to wallpaper in that it brings pattern and texture to your walls, fabric is another option available for creating a decorative wall treatment. Fabric is ideal for camouflaging less-than-perfect walls and is reminiscent of the days when tapestries were hung on walls both for decoration and as a buffer against cold drafts. Ideally, fabric should be put in place by a professional who can attach fabric to walls with staples or create an elegant shirred effect with rods.

A handsome wooden wainscot has long been a favorite wall treatment in a traditional decor. Solid wood boards are applied to the bottom third of the wall and capped with a chair rail or decorative molding. A wainscot can be painted, stained, or simply varnished. In a formal living room, nothing rivals the beauty and understated good looks of wood, and a wainscot also contributes subtle architectural embellishment.

Where a more generous wood treatment is desired, walls can be paneled. During the eighteenth century and early nineteenth century, it was common practice to panel the fireplace wall, but an entire room can be paneled to create a living room that also functions as a library or home office. Depending upon the color and type of wood used for paneling, you can create a handsome, masculine setting or a living room with a casual, rustic ambience that brings to mind a country retreat.

Floor Treatments

What's underfoot is every bit as important as what's on the walls in the traditional living room. A period or classic decor calls upon the past without giving up the comfort and easy-care options of the present. A hardwood floor is—and always has been—favored for its strength, beauty, and the elegant patina that only time can create. For a variation on a wood floor, a parquet floor in a classic herringbone pattern is simply stunning, adding a formal air to the living room. An exquisite Oriental rug can create a focal point or define a conversation area and elevate the effect to one of stately beauty.

Other types of rugs at home in a traditional decor include needlepoint (which have been popular since the 1700s), those with floral or geometric motifs, and French Aubusson rugs, revered for their formal center medallion designs. When looking at rugs, remember that antiques will be quite costly, but excellent reproductions are available that will serve you well for many years. Buy an area rug from someone who specializes in them and can assure you of the materials and technique used to produce the rug.

While a wood floor can be left bare, the addition of one or more area rugs can be the ideal finishing touch, regardless of whether your living room is formal or informal. The colors, designs, and textures available make rugs a wonderful companion in a room full of neoclassical furnishings, period pieces, or even laid-back, airy wicker.

Wall-to-wall carpeting is another flooring option, one that's both practical and beautiful. The traditional living room can be enhanced by the color and texture of room-size carpeting. Once again, there are so many hues available that carpeting can easily be chosen to match any color scheme. A light-toned carpet will help open up a small space, but for a larger room consider a deep shade to create a more intimate feeling. From a practical standpoint, carpeting provides warmth underfoot, and most brands are treated for soil and stain resistance.

Wool is the most luxurious and costly kind of carpeting. Man-made materials, such as acrylic, nylon, and polyester, are also used in carpet manufacturing, and nylon is noted for its durability and woollike qualities. Be aware that carpeting is produced in several different ways and the key factor is whether the carpet pile is cut or uncut. Different piles offer different looks. In a formal setting, consider using a cut and loop to emphasize pattern, a plush carpet to convey richness, or a multilevel loop for a sculptured effect. A level loop carpet or an Axminster is ideal in a more casual room.

ABOVE: Soft colors and elegant furnishings combine to create a simple yet lovely living room reminiscent of the early Victorian age. A striking neoclassical settee fits perfectly in the shuttered alcove, where it is bathed in diffused light. An Oriental area rug plays up the handsome wood floor, while a vintage hanging light fixture reinforces the period theme.

✧✧✧

ABOVE: Period style is apparent everywhere in this Victorian parlor. Subtly papered walls, a decorative plaster ceiling, and a painted plank floor accessorized with area rugs surround Rococo Revival–style furnishings upholstered in luxurious burgundy velvet. A corner whatnot shelf displays a collection of delicate china, and a lace-dressed center table is the ideal spot for a cup of tea.

ABOVE: A lovely patterned room-size rug and ornate window treatments are fitting accessories for a living room that combines a medley of furniture styles. Painted and inlaid wooden pieces give the room a timeless appeal, while slipcovered and upholstered chairs add more casual comfort. Decorative accents, such as twin mirrors, floral bouquets, and favorite collectibles, lend a distinctly personal touch.

Window Treatments

Windows can be yet another decorative element in the traditional living room, and they offer a multitude of options when it comes to creating beauty and elegance. While attention to detail has long been a hallmark of classic style, there are times when a simplified window dressing—or no dressing at all—can make a fabulous statement. For example, a living room in which handsome furnishings are the focal point can benefit from an unassuming window treatment that still retains a measure of timeless style. A living room where windows contribute architectural panache or provide a panoramic view can be treated with a minimalist approach. The majority of living rooms, however, will benefit from a decorative window treatment that complements a traditional decor.

In a more formal setting, floor-length draperies made of damask, silk, velvet, brocade, taffeta, or linen are an excellent choice when dealing with tall windows. Remember that draperies should be lined to protect expensive fabric from the sun. Once hung, draperies can be looped back to the side of the window with a decorative rope, braids and tassels, or metal clips designed with a classical motif. Adding a valance, swag and jabot, or fabric-covered cornice gives the formal window treatment a polished look.

Choosing the color and/or pattern for draperies will be determined by the colors featured in the living room, especially the furniture upholstery. Plain fabrics can be made dressy with a fabric trim, braiding, or fringe in a contrasting color. If patterned drapery is called for, subtle stripes are always at home in a traditional decor, as are large floral patterns and toile de Jouy. For something a bit more opulent, especially in a high-style parlor that takes its cue from the Victorian age, a window dressing with layers of fabric is ideal. You might want to consider pairing a lace undercurtain with a rich velvet drapery.

A toned-down window dressing is perfect in a small living room, especially one with smaller windows. Simplicity, too, is associated with many of the traditional homes during the eighteenth and early nineteenth centuries. For a semiformal or casual mood, a floral chintz window dressing is always a welcome addition to the living room. Satin, sheers, or ticking are other simple yet lovely options. Also consider using elegant hardware to show off your drapes. Metal poles for case-headed drapes come in a variety of painted finishes, and finials are available with such classic designs as urns, balls, or pineapples (which have long been associated with the Colonial home and

were a popular stencil design for walls). An understated drapery can be looped back or pulled to one side, or a length of fabric can be used as a tailed swag at a window that doesn't require a full dressing for privacy.

Room shades can be used with drapes in a traditional setting, or for a minimalist scheme, they can be used alone to provide a tailored look. Roman shades are a bit more formal, and can be made with pleats for a more decorative approach to window dressing.

Handsome wooden shutters are often used in tandem with draperies in a traditional living room. Paint them to match walls or woodwork for a subtle look, or allow a rich wood finish to convey warmth and masculine appeal.

Lace panels are a lovely accent in a period room that calls upon the Arts and Crafts movement for its sense of style. Juxtaposed with linear oak furnishings, art glass lamps, and a beautiful Oriental rug, lace curtains add a soft touch and filter light.

⟨≥×≤⟩

OPPOSITE: Large living rooms can be made more cozy and intimate by arranging furniture into different conversation areas rather than placing pieces symmetrically along the walls. Here, a neoclassical side chair and upholstered easy chair create a place to relax in front of a gallery of Asian artwork. The dramatic length of the draw curtains turns a simple window treatment into an elegant one.

ABOVE: This striking living room benefits from an exceptionally tall ceiling and a light-filled wall of windows. Airy fabric is swagged across a decorative curtain rod for a dressy effect, while a beautiful pier glass is positioned above the mantel. Comfortable upholstered chairs and window seats provide plenty of opportunity for relaxation, and two small tea tables serve in place of a coffee table. A neutral color scheme allows the architectural features to shine.

Lighting

Windows naturally function to allow light into the living room, but they need a helping hand on overcast days and in the evening, when artificial light sources are needed. Generally, lighting is thought of in terms of accent, task, and general lighting. The majority of living rooms will include a mixture of all three types.

Accent lighting in a traditional living room often takes the form of wall sconces. Sconces, which can focus light either up or down, are often used as a decorative element. They are also used to spotlight architectural embellishments (such as a handsome overmantel) and select artwork or antiques. Candlestick-style sconces with miniature fabric shades are ideal in a formal setting, while brass sconces with delicate glass shades find their way into a more casual or semiformal setting.

Task lighting illuminates a specific area so that you can comfortably accomplish the task or hobby at hand, which in the living room is likely to be reading or perhaps working on a craft project. Table and floor lamps are the most common examples of task lighting, but don't let the name fool you—lamps used to brighten a work area can be a striking decorative addition to the classic beauty of the living room. Table lamps are available with a wide assortment of lovely bases, and there are more than enough shade styles to choose from. Timeless designs include the ginger-jar lamp, the candlestick lamp, and the urn-shaped lamp.

The ginger-jar lamp can be quite simple or elaborate, have a metal or ceramic base, and feature a solid color or a painted design. Ginger-jar lamps with Oriental motifs are especially at home in a traditional decor. For good measure, a white or colored pleated shade adds a handsome, tailored look. In contrast to the rounded design of the ginger-jar lamp, the candlestick style is tall and slender, and is available in assorted colors with plain or patterned shades. Urn-shaped lamps are reminiscent of ancient cultures and are quite fitting in a living room that pays tribute to neoclassical designs.

Numerous other possibilities exist in regard to table lamps. A copper-based lamp with an art glass shade is a must in an Arts and Crafts–inspired living room, while lamps with floral chintz shades (ideally coordinated with upholstery or draperies) are at home in a Victorian setting.

General or background lighting calls for something more substantial—perhaps a period perfect chandelier that will cast a soft glow throughout the living room. Another option is recessed lighting, which is unobtrusive enough to be used with virtually any decor. Ideally, a chandelier or recessed lighting should be operated by a dimmer switch so that you can control the level of lighting in the living room.

⬧⬧⬧

OPPOSITE: This elegant living room, furnished with a striking upholstered chaise longue, plump easy chair, and wire armchair, is cast in a soft glow courtesy of recessed lighting and a brass floor lamp. A beautiful wooden chest, an elegant mirror, and a window treatment that echoes the colors and pattern displayed in the area rug give the room a polished look. ABOVE: A unique pole lamp, books, and select collectibles help fashion a cozy spot for reading. Even the smallest decorative detail can convey traditional style, such as the tassel that embellishes this divan. Incorporating throw pillows that echo the colors in the wallpaper, this room takes on a classic and coordinated look.

◇⊰⊱◇

OPPOSITE: The formal spirit of this living room calls for elegant lighting. Symmetrically placed candlestick lamps grace a lovely table ideal for displaying select items. Behind the sofa, an urn-shaped lamp with a pleated shade provides task lighting for reading and enhances the room's decor.

ABOVE: A rustic board-and-batten wall treatment and the whimsical folk-art painting that holds a proud place above the marble-topped chest bring formal country style to this living room. Wall-hung cupids and a miniature birdhouse are fitting accessories, as are the canine figurines, matching candlesticks, and beautiful porcelain lamp with a patterned fabric shade.

Furnishings

Fine details and solid comfort are imperative in a traditional decorating scheme. With this in mind, what is the best approach to furnishing the living room? Of course you should consider the styles of the past, but take into account your current needs as well. Call upon your personal style to guide you toward a living room that will serve you and your family well for years to come. Invest in quality furnishings (whether antiques or reproductions) that exhibit fine craftsmanship and timeless beauty.

Upholstered pieces are fitting for a classic look. The fine lines of a traditional sofa (such as a camel-back, straight-back, or wood-trimmed antique) will help set the balance and proportion of the space. A sofa of standard height, usually fourteen to eighteen inches (35.5 to 46cm), is preferred in the living room—save the overstuffed couch for the family room.

Furniture construction should be a major concern when investing in a new sofa. Look for hardwood frames, and take note of the joinery method that's been used. A sofa that employs a series of dowels will last longer than one simply nailed together. Also, try to choose a sofa with coil springs, since they will provide optimum comfort and longevity.

The fabric chosen for a traditional sofa will depend upon whether you're trying to achieve a formal or a more casual look. Rich woven fabrics include brocade, damask, and tapestry. Brocade features a raised pattern, while damask is identified by a flat pattern. Both are available in a variety of colors and designs. Tapestry is a heavy fabric that's easily identified by its strong use of colors and graphics, such as scenic designs or the flame-stitch pattern.

Keep the watchwords "attention to detail" in mind when choosing a sofa for a formal living room. Elegant touches, such as a fringed or tailored skirt, carved woodwork, or tasseled pillows, will enhance a sofa's classic character.

In the traditional-inspired living room where you want to be able to let your hair down and put your feet up, opt for upholstery that's durable but no less desirable than richer materials. Fine examples include corduroy, jacquard, hopsack, ticking, tweed, or light canvas. Made from linen, cotton, cotton blends, or wool blends, these sturdy fabrics are available in a range of colors and designs to suit any decorating scheme.

Along with the sofa, a variety of chairs will contribute to the comfort level of a traditional living room. Consider a classic wing chair or two, or perhaps an upholstered armchair with a matching ottoman. Add a selection

LEFT: This pale yellow living room is beautifully furnished and accessorized with formal, traditional pieces. A floral rug defines the conversation area before the hearth, where a tailored sofa, fringed ottoman, and upholstered open armchairs provide comfortable seating. A round table sporting a classic ginger-jar lamp is bedecked with a blue and yellow striped fabric that just happens to match the lovely window drapes. Note, too, how the built-in bookcases provide ample display space for cherished mementos.

OPPOSITE: Handsome and rugged, this living room decor takes its cue from the vaulted wood-beamed ceiling, brick hearth, and stunning array of windows. Casual country ambience is achieved by blending comfy upholstered furnishings with a medley of wooden tables and an eye-catching desk. A large floral bouquet, plenty of throw pillows, and family photos on display add old-fashioned warmth and appeal.

LEFT: This well-appointed living room has a lighthearted elegance thanks to the gold and white color palette. The dressy draperies, as well as the matching valance, are trimmed in the same bold stripe used on the upholstered furnishings and are looped back with gold tassels. Formality is tempered, however, with a decorative fabric-covered screen, a unique standing lamp, and a folk-art table with a scalloped apron.

OPPOSITE: A beautiful armoire holds a place of honor between the tall windows in this softly hued living room. Buff walls create a soothing background for a white overstuffed sofa and matching armchairs. The handsome, dark wooden coffee table, recalling the substantial furnishings designed in the neoclassical Empire style, is ideal for displaying fresh blossoms and a silver candlestick.

of side chairs (with or without arms) to provide different types of seating. Chairs of various period designs can be mixed, and this will enhance the character of your room. If you're smitten by the Colonial era, choose Queen Anne or Chippendale armchairs, which feature upholstered seats in a stunning brocade, cotton print, or damask. Floral or striped patterns play nicely against the richness of walnut, mahogany, or cherry wood. If, on the other hand, neoclassical styles are your passion, Federal or Empire armchairs (Hepplewhite or Sheraton) that display the stately elegance of delicate lyre-back or shield-back designs will give your living room a classical ambience. For a traditional living room with strong country roots, Windsor chairs, French Provençal armchairs with rush seats, or straightforward Shaker-style chairs contribute more of a rustic flavor. Balloon-back chairs have strong ties to the Victorian age, and the William Morris reclining chair is ideal in an Arts and Crafts setting.

In addition to seating, you'll want to include a variety of other pieces in the living room that will be both beautiful and functional. While many are apt to think that a handsome chest of drawers belongs in the bedroom, tradition tells us they were initially found in the "parlor" or best room in the homes of long ago. And it makes perfect sense: why hide a magnificent period chest when it can be put to use in the living room as a focal point, a place to display a tablescape, and a convenient storage area? Consider the possibilities of including a bombé, serpentine-front, or bow-front chest of drawers in the traditional living room. Not only is there enough space for a tabletop lamp, a floral display, or a cluster of treasured objects, but drawer space can be used to hide linens, magazines, and photo albums. Such a chest is ideal in a small living room where space is a premium.

Other case pieces, such as a large Queen Anne highboy or a Chippendale chest-on-chest, can be striking in the living room. Keep balance and proportion in mind, since both case pieces are substantial furnishings and could easily dominate a room.

Most living rooms require assorted tables to assure adequate space for tabletop lamps and books, or for resting a cup of tea. Again, let your personal style guide you. Don't overlook the possibilities of placing a drop-leaf table against a living room wall, where it can be used as a spot to do paperwork or host an intimate dinner for two. In today's home, rooms as well as furnishings are often called upon to do double duty. And sometimes the unexpected turns out to be the perfect decorating solution. Rather than a long coffee

table, why not try two tea tables placed side by side in front of the sofa? A bamboo tray table can also serve as a coffee table and contributes a nice touch of Oriental flair. For those drawn to upholstered pieces, an ottoman can easily be used as a coffee table by outfitting it with a lovely tray to steady drinks or dishes. Even a handsome wooden chest can act as a table in a casual living room, with the added benefit of providing storage for games and magazines. Actually, your possibilities are almost limitless. Consider the size of your room and decide upon those furniture pieces that will meet your needs while providing a comfortable, inviting surrounding.

Regardless of whether the furniture you love calls to mind age-old English styles or exhibits French or country influences, the manner in which you arrange your furniture speaks volumes about your personal style. Formal settings are typically created by placing furniture along walls in a symmetrical fashion. While this is fine in a smaller space, it can make a large living room seem cold and austere. Instead, consider grouping furniture in several conversation areas to make the room seem more intimate. For a casual air, arrange furniture around a focal point, such as a fireplace.

Accessories

Details truly do make all the difference, and nowhere is this more apparent than in the decorative accessories you choose for your traditional living room. They should make both a stylistic and a personal statement. If you love art and have collected such pieces as antique botanical prints, architectural etchings, or vintage portraits, by all means, show them off. Play up their artistic merit by using a bracket-mounted art lamp to draw attention to favorite examples. Also, give considerable thought to the frames as well as the artwork. While substantial gilt frames have long been favored in a traditional setting, you may prefer the warmth of a wood finish or the understated elegance of an ebony frame. Smaller works of art or a collection of family photographs can be placed in brass or silver frames. A symmetrical display of artwork is typical in a traditional decor, but you may want to experiment by placing the pieces at various heights to create an interesting wallscape.

Mirrors are associated with a traditional decor and are especially at home in the living room, where they've been used since the eighteenth century. They can still work their magic by making firelight or candlelight dance and reflecting light in a soft glow. Today, period mirrors are being reproduced in a number of styles, and some display architectural qualities admired for their classic appeal. Place a handsome mirror above the mantel, over a pier table, or situated between two windows.

Collections can become an important part of a decorating scheme. Furnishings are often selected specifically to show them off, and sometimes rooms are planned around them. Imagine how beautiful a mantel can appear when a collection of silver candlesticks is grouped together and the candles are lit to cast a warm glow. Or perhaps a bombé chest is home to several porcelain jars collected on trips abroad. Built-in bookcases can be a showplace for leather-bound classics that are read over and over again. A tabletop can be the perfect place to display small but treasured items and perhaps a bouquet of beautiful flowers.

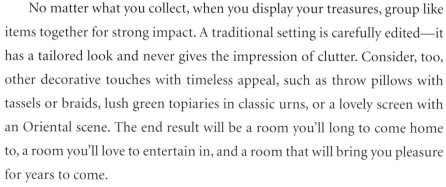

No matter what you collect, when you display your treasures, group like items together for strong impact. A traditional setting is carefully edited—it has a tailored look and never gives the impression of clutter. Consider, too, other decorative touches with timeless appeal, such as throw pillows with tassels or braids, lush green topiaries in classic urns, or a lovely screen with an Oriental scene. The end result will be a room you'll long to come home to, a room you'll love to entertain in, and a room that will bring you pleasure for years to come.

OPPOSITE: Initially favored for its ability to reflect candlelight during the evening hours, the mirror became a status symbol of sorts in the eighteenth-century home, and has remained popular through the years. Atop a mantel, above a pier table, or positioned on a prominent living room wall, a wood-framed or gilt-trimmed mirror is a hallmark of traditional style. This lovely example is well suited to a small alcove that accommodates a tailored love seat.

ABOVE: Vibrant colors and a well-edited collection of paintings and collectibles give this living room timeless appeal. Upholstered open armchairs by the hearth and a soft blue sofa encourage relaxation. A beautiful Oriental rug anchors the room and contributes a touch of formality. Traditional blue and white china, porcelain figurines, and unique handcrafted vases express the owners' love of fine pottery.

THE DINING ROOM

The dining room as we know it today did not really become common in homes until the middle of the nineteenth century. Prior to that time, family meals were often served in the kitchen near the warmth of the hearth, or the parlor or sitting room doubled as a dining area for the evening meal. Any number of tables would do: a Queen Anne drop-leaf table, which usually stood against the sitting room wall, could be moved to the center of the room and side chairs pulled into place. In town houses, this combination sitting and dining room was located in the basement because of its close proximity to the kitchen.

The wealthy may have preferred the drawing room or formal parlor for an elegant meal, especially if guests were expected. It was not unusual for a neoclassical-style sideboard, various side tables, and possibly a built-in corner cupboard to be included in the parlor so that when meals did indeed take place there, everything was close at hand.

Preparing the parlor or sitting room for dinner entailed rearranging the furniture. The symmetrical placement of chairs and side tables along walls kept the center of the room available for setting up the dining table. The first priority was covering the area rug or carpet with a protective crumb cloth made of wool, canvas, or green baize. Since Oriental and other types of rugs were quite costly and constituted a sizable investment for the average family, it made perfect sense to protect them from possible spills or crumbs.

Once the crumb cloth was in place, the table was situated atop it and the numerous Queen Anne, Chippendale, Windsor, or neoclassical side chairs that stood about the room were arranged for seating at the table. The table itself was covered with a crisp white cloth that hung down on all sides, and pewter or china dinnerware was set at each place. At the end of the meal, the furnishings were returned to their proper places, the crumb cloth was removed, and the dining room once again became the parlor or sitting room.

OPPOSITE: A beautiful harvest table and bright yellow and white rush-seat French country chairs furnish this appealing dining room. Decorative touches, such as the tiled hearth, wood-beamed ceiling, and metal wall sconces, add to the regional style. The collection of blue and white dishes on the wall above the fireplace pays tribute to the past.
ABOVE: A delicate neoclassical table and chairs provide a place for gourmet dinners or everyday pleasures, such as a cup of coffee and the daily paper. The Colonial-era sideboard is both practical and decorative, with a handsome plate rack to display dishes and space to store papers and magazines. A beautiful arrangement of autumn leaves and an Oriental rug enhance the room's warmth and beauty.

By the 1840s, dining had become a social activity, and having a separate dining room became an important measure of status and gentility. Victorian architectural plan books usually included a dining room on the first floor of the home, across the center hall from the parlor. With this new status symbol came the introduction of an important and specialized furnishing especially for the dining room—the massive sideboard.

The sideboard of the Victorian era differed from its neoclassical counterpart in that it was intended for display more so than for storage or ease in serving meals. A Federal sideboard was a long case piece on thin, tall legs, with small drawers for cutlery and two or more small cupboards for linens. In contrast, legs virtually disappeared on the Victorian sideboard, and while storage space was available in the form of bottom cupboards, the most important feature was the handsome wood or marble top and shelves that proved ideal for the display of fine china, crystal, and sterling objects.

These massive sideboards were also ornately embellished with carvings, scrollwork, or incised lines. In essence they set the tone of the mid- to late-nineteenth-century dining room, where displaying the owner's beautiful dinnerware was as important as serving meals of refined elegance. And it didn't take long before social reformers and domestic science authorities of the day began to protest the excess associated with the dining room of the late 1800s. They called for simplified, less labor-intensive meals, as well as a more modest setting. The obvious display of wealth was increasingly viewed as inappropriate, and as a result, simpler furnishings and toned-down decorating schemes were in vogue by the dawn of the twentieth century.

Although many of the homes constructed during the early 1900s featured an open floor plan, the dining room never actually went out of style. It has remained steadfast in the majority of North American homes and today, as in days past, may actually serve a dual purpose. Consider the traditional dining room outfitted with shelves to house a collection of books.

ABOVE: Natural wood tones add a rustic element to this beguiling dining area, while delicate carving provides elegance. In a unique interpretation of traditional style, wainscoting and borders are carved into the planks that form the walls. The ornate design of the mirror frame complements the decorative work on the buffet and the chair backs.

OPPOSITE: A handsome side board is placed against a striking red wall in this gracious dining room. Outfitted with a decorative ginger-jap lamp, a silver coffee service, and a bouquet of fresh flowers, this display makes a stunning vignette. The gilt-framed painting of a spaniel adds just a hint of formality, as do the fringed draperies tied back with cord and tassels.

❦❧

OPPOSITE: Dressed for a holiday celebration, this charming dining room is a study in red and white. Metal heart-back chairs surround a lovely table set with elegant china and draped with layers of fabric. The ledge running along the walls is ideal for displaying porcelain jars and seasonal greens, and the mirrored half-wall makes the room appear larger. Even the crystal chandelier is decorated with holly and silver balls for the holiday festivities.

ABOVE: In the nineteenth century, dark red walls were popular in the dining room because the color was thought to aid digestion. Here, a lovely cranberry-colored wall proves a warm backdrop for period furnishings and a decorative shelf with a plate rack. In keeping with the color scheme, a beautiful red and white fabric has been selected for matching side chairs that can be pulled to the table for dinner guests. The buffet showcases a medley of china and allows plenty of room for a delicate spray of flowers and a hand-painted porcelain lamp.

Or perhaps your dining room is the perfect place to do work brought home from the office. In fact, it may even serve as a home office, with a computer and accessories hidden behind the doors of a lovely armoire.

Whether you have a formal dining room or a dining space carved out of an intimate corner in the living room, a traditional decor will create a comfortable, elegant, and welcome spot for treasured family meals or gatherings with friends. Look first to color as a key element in creating the perfect backdrop. Often the color you choose will depend upon whether you're dealing with a separate room or a dining space adjoining the kitchen or living room. During the nineteenth century, deep hues were preferred in the dining room, since they were thought to have a calming effect that aided digestion. Colors such as crimson, magenta, or fern green were often used in dining rooms, and while these same colors can be striking in a traditional decor today, pastels are also suitable in a formal setting. Bold primary colors are generally reserved for a casual dining room, and neutrals can be dressed up or down to achieve a formal or semiformal tone.

Wall Treatments

Paint is an obvious choice for a wall treatment if your dining area is an extension of other living spaces. That doesn't mean, however, that it can't be set apart. A wallpaper border, chair rail, or wainscoting used in tandem with paint can create focus and define the space. A separate dining room, on the other hand, allows more flexibility for a total departure from other color schemes used throughout the house. Walls can be painted in your favorite hue—be it sunny yellow or deep blue—and woodwork can be given an elegant lift with a crisp coat of white paint.

A decorative paint effect can lend subtle beauty to dining room walls. For something a bit different, you may want to consider color washing, which can give walls a soft, aged look. Three or more shades of a watered-down color are applied with random brush strokes, layer upon layer, with the end result being walls that convey old-world elegance.

Marbling as a decorative effect can be quite striking in a stately dining room. Walls are painted to imitate marble by applying the appropriate base coat and then using colored wax crayons to draw marks. The marks are then softened out with a brush, and a coat of varnish is applied. Both color washing and marbling take some practice to achieve the desired results. It's a good idea to contact a professional for such work, or at the very least refer to books published on the subject for detailed instructions and a complete listing of the necessary paints and tools.

Wallpaper, of course, can be lovely in a traditional dining room. With so many patterns available, you should have no problem finding the perfect color and pattern for a formal or casual space given over to the pleasure of enjoyable meals, relaxation, and good company. Consider narrowing your

ABOVE: This dining room has been made inviting with warm plank flooring, dark green wallpaper
bearing a subtle striped pattern, and a white tongue-and-groove ceiling. Casual elegance is achieved by
juxtaposing a pine harvest table with upholstered medallion-back chairs that wear a medley of soft
prints. A countrified hutch displays favorite dishes, while the light area rug, floral curtains, and
gilt-framed paintings reinforce the traditional decorating scheme.

ABOVE: An artfully painted round table is joined by neoclassical chairs with blue and white striped cushions in this small dining area. The backdrop is decidedly Victorian—a striped wallpaper dado is separated from a trellis-patterned field by a chair rail. Framed floral prints and dark green balloon shades add a soft touch.

ABOVE: Old-world style, always a class act, makes this dining room an enjoyable place to linger. A timeworn table that just gets better with age is surrounded by a casual mix of chairs. The dark timbered ceiling, yellow plaster walls, and wrought-iron chandelier are cozy and reminiscent of an English cottage. Blue is used as an accent color—for the dishes, the picture frames, and even the flowers.

options to the tried-and-true: a floral pattern in a crewelwork design, an Oriental motif, a scenic pattern, stripes, or perhaps a motif of gold stars on a colored background. A French Provençal floral pattern would be ideal in a dining area with European or high-style country roots, and a beautiful flocked paper (with a raised pattern to imitate fabric) would convey Victoriana in a dining room that looks to the mid-nineteenth century for stylistic inspiration. For the dining room that takes its cue from the Arts and Crafts movement, a stylized floral wallpaper in the fine tradition of William Morris is unsurpassed. Whatever pattern you choose, you also have the option of incorporating a matching or complementary fabric to give chair seats and draperies a tailored effect.

Dining room walls can be papered in their entirety or combined with paint or wainscoting for a division of space. Or wallpaper can be used sparingly to display select touches of creativity. For example, if you love the look of wallpaper but are hesitant to commit to covering your walls in full, consider stunning wallpaper panels. Painted with a handsome wooden

wainscot, the upper portion of dining room walls can be divided into panels defined by classic moldings, with the area between moldings papered. Not only does this infuse the traditional dining room with pattern, but it lends significant architectural interest as well.

Trompe l'oeil (meaning "to fool the eye") has frequently been used as a decorative paint effect, but precut wallpaper examples are of such high quality that it is difficult to tell paint from paper. A grand design can be incorporated into a formal dining room via architectural columns, classic urns, and even statues. By combining a tromp l'oeil design with a scenic wallpaper, for example, walls become an artistic tribute as well as a visual feast.

For something a bit less obvious, a wallpaper border can be used as a frieze just below the ceiling. Opt for an embossed border that has the look of molded plasterwork, and it becomes an instant classical detail. A border can also be used in place of a molded chair rail or as a "frame" to embellish the placement of a wall mirror or a notable piece of artwork.

Floor Treatments

In today's traditional dining room, floors are treated much as they are in the living room. Wall-to-wall carpeting, especially high-quality rugs treated for stain resistance, will contribute solid comfort and a sense of unity. For a richer look, a carpeted dining room floor can be "layered" or accessorized with a beautiful Oriental or needlepoint rug to define the table area.

Traditionally considered a bit more casual, a sisal rug can be used instead of plush carpeting in the dining room. Today, a sisal rug is equally at home in a dressed-up room done in neutrals or earth tones and in a more relaxed setting that has a country air. Once found primarily in bedrooms and summer homes, modern-day sisal carpeting is now being used throughout the house with surprising and elegant results.

Hardwood floors have long been featured in the dining room for their warmth and handsome looks. A uniform wood floor and a decorative parquet floor are still excellent options today in a traditional setting. For extra polish, an area rug can be added.

For the dining room with country flair or old-world, casual charm, a wide plank softwood flooring (such as pine) may be more to your liking. This type of flooring is enhanced by age and develops a soft patina that adds a rustic elegance to the dining area. Lay down a floral or geometric needlepoint rug for added comfort and design interest.

ABOVE: This inviting dining room has a casual country air, thanks to the stylish combination of a
light-colored wooden table and dark-hued wooden ladder-back chairs with decorative spool turnings.
The beamed ceiling and terra-cotta floor add rugged texture. The windows have been left bare to
take advantage of a leafy green view. A wooden rack filled with flowers and whimsical
carved giraffes add to the charm.

Lighting

Lighting in a dining room with classic appeal calls for a chandelier situated about thirty inches (76cm) above the table (unless you have unusually high ceilings). To adequately control the level of lighting, a dimmer switch should be included. Naturally the type of chandelier you choose will be influenced by the style of your furnishings and the room's ambience. A crystal chandelier with sparkling prisms will complement the formality and elegance of a handsome Chippendale table and chairs, but it may be a little too heavy-handed in the dining room outfitted with a nondescript table and Windsor chairs. Or perhaps not—after all, juxtaposition can work decorating marvels. There are numerous styles to select from, including chandeliers with mini candlestick lamps and shades, brass pendant lights, metal fixtures with the look of antique iron, and lamps with beautiful glass shades.

Wall sconces can add attractive accent lighting in a traditional dining room. Sconces come in a wide variety of designs and styles. They can be positioned to flank a classic sideboard, a large mirror, a beautiful painting, or a fireplace overmantel. In lieu of sconces, a beautiful torchère placed in the corner of a small dining room can serve the same purpose.

Candlelight and elegant dinners go hand in hand, so silver, brass, pewter, or glass candlesticks and candelabras are right at home in the traditional dining room. Place them on the table, the sideboard, the mantel, and wherever else you have space to display a collection.

ABOVE: Lighting in the traditional dining room can include chandeliers, wall sconces, table-top lamps on the buffet or sideboard, and of course, candles. During the evening, this lovely room is bathed in the soft, dancing light from the candles in the beautiful wrought-iron chandelier. This chandelier is the perfect counterpoint to the urn-shaped lamps resting on the exquisite twin Victorian pier tables.

OPPOSITE: Color-washed plaster walls and the rustic textures of the timbered ceiling and tile floor play host to a beautiful rectangular table and matching side chairs that recall Queen Anne style. The soft reds and golds of this room are contrasted with select touches of blue—most noticeably in the striking wrought-iron chandelier and matching wall sconce.

Window Treatments

Next, turn your attention to the windows. Does the tone of your traditional dining room call for a sophisticated and elegant drapery treatment, or will something simpler, such as a lovely valance, be more in keeping with your personal style? In a separate dining room, windows can be dressed without concern for coordinating the treatment with other areas of your home. If, however, your dining space is an extension of the living room, you'll want a unified look.

A stately dining room with formal styling benefits from a stunning and decorative drapery treatment. Texture and pattern are as important as color, and fabrics such as brocade, satin, damask, or taffeta are ideal for a rich effect. In contrast, draperies made of linen or floral chintz are less formal but every bit as lovely. Chintz is a popular choice in a traditional dining room when you want to match the draperies with the upholstery. While it's not a heavy-duty fabric, chintz is well suited to dining room chairs that don't receive a lot of hard use.

Draperies can be enhanced with a valance or fabric-covered cornice. In a formal dining room where you desire a focus on pattern, try mixing a subtle striped drapery with a floral valance in corresponding colors. A valance is also the perfect touch in a dining room with

a Victorian decorating theme. If, however, you prefer draperies without a valance, choose decorative hardware to supply the perfect finishing touch, and consider using elegant metal or fabric-covered rods with finials sporting a classical design.

Traditional dining rooms that tend to be a bit more casual, especially those rooms that offer a lovely view, may require a window treatment only as a detail and not necessarily as a full window covering. A simple swag or a combination swag and jabot may be all that's called for. By adding a sumptuous fringe or tassels to swags, valances, jabots, or drapes, you can heighten the visual appeal of your window treatment.

Sheer or lace curtains are a delicate addition in a dining area where the focus is on furnishings and the background remains neutral. They are also the preferred window treatment in an Arts and Crafts–period room, where the design aesthetic has always emphasized simplicity, beauty, and fine craftsmanship.

Fabric, wood, or vinyl blinds are popular options for directing natural lighting, and while these are often thought of as contemporary, with careful selection of material and color they can be used in a traditional setting with pleasing results. The color chosen for fabric blinds can be coordinated with draperies, or a handsome wood blind can be used with a swag and jabot to create the illusion of architectural embellishment. And speaking of wood, shutters can also be used in the dining room. Paint them white to match woodwork, or play up wood tones with a dark stain. Shutters are highly versatile—they can be equally at home in a formal or casual setting.

OPPOSITE: This intimate dining room illustrates the romantic side of traditional style. A round table draped with pale gold and white linen tablecloths is dressed up with lace-edged napkins. Delicate Empire-style chairs enhance the room's classic appeal. Narrow built-in bookcases, well suited to a dining room that serves multiple functions, keep books close at hand without making the room look cluttered. Notice how the textured white area rug and print tab curtains on a lovely metal rod subtly contribute to the ambience.
LEFT: A spacious enclosed porch makes the perfect setting for fine dining. The wonderful view is the focal point here, so the furnishings are kept simple. An understated but lovely table is casually draped with a fern-patterned linen cloth and surrounded by a medley of Windsor and neoclassical chairs painted white. A candle-filled chandelier with curved metal arms will provide soft lighting once evening arrives, and the roses, of course, will scent the night air.

Furnishings

When it comes to furnishing your traditional dining room, does your personal style guide you toward pieces with soft, graceful curves, or do you prefer clean, straight lines? Do you admire the gleam of handsome dark woods, such as walnut or mahogany, or are inlay patterns more to your liking? Do you feel most comfortable surrounded by large, masculine pieces, or are you drawn to delicate, small-scale furnishings? These are just a few of the questions you should consider before investing in antique or fine reproduction furnishings for a room that is generally given over to entertaining and family affairs.

You'll also want to keep in mind the size of your dining area. If it's a large room and you have a big family or like to entertain often, a sizable table (or one that can be extended) is ideal. If, on the other hand, your dining space is on the small side, or if it doubles as a home office or work area, a compromise is definitely called for.

Last but far from least, what tone will your traditional dining room set: formal, semiformal, or casual? Since furniture is a major investment and

something you will live with for years, be sure it meets your needs in terms of style, size, function, and comfort. Undoubtedly the sideboard was the focal point in the dining room during the nineteenth century, but times have changed, and today the spotlight is on your table and chairs. For a period look, a mahogany, cherry, or walnut Queen Anne or Chippendale dining set can give your room a formal mood. Pull upholstered wing chairs up to the table at either end for dramatic impact and additional comfort. If space allows, a beautiful high chest, chest-on-chest, or period chest of drawers will provide a place to store linens and silverware and will grace your room with timeless appeal.

A semiformal or casual mood can be achieved by introducing the old-world elegance of French Provençal furnishings. A handsome table, slat-back chairs with upholstered or rush seats, and a substantial armoire for storage can combine to form a stunning backdrop that makes use of traditional French fabrics and patterns.

A country-style room can be elegantly furnished with a long harvest table and Windsor chairs. If you prefer a minimalist approach to a country-inspired decor, a Shaker table and slat-back chairs are reminiscent of the simplicity that served as a way of life for many eighteenth- and nineteenth-century religious followers.

For classical appeal in a traditional dining room, consider Federal- or Empire-style furnishings. Choose an oval or rectangular table accompanied by shield-back chairs or chairs that display urn-shaped splats or lyre backs. The sideboard made its debut during the early neoclassical period, and one in the Federal style with inlay decorations and mahogany veneer is a fitting addition to a formal setting.

A timeless ambience can also be created in the dining area by evoking the spirit of a style in subtle ways. In place of an elongated dining room table, especially when space is at a premium, consider using a round table covered with elegant layers of fabric, and then outfit this with two or four faux bamboo chairs for a salute to Oriental design. Or substitute period or classical-style chairs to create a different look.

Just as the dining room often served more than one purpose in homes of the past, today's dining room can do double duty as a home library or office. With so many people working out of the home today, it makes perfect sense for us to optimize our use of space and do it with style. Built-in bookcases or handsome shelves

The opulent beauty of a Victorian-period room often implies excessive ornamentation and embellishment. While this can be true, it doesn't always have to be so. A Rococo Revival–style table and upholstered balloon-back chairs can be elegant by themselves without an overdressed background. Add a period sideboard to display dining room accessories and then tone down—or up—your walls, windows, and floor. In an Arts and Crafts setting, Mission oak or oak look-alike furnishings will convey this period style, but your background can be made subtle with pastel walls or played up with a vibrant wallpaper.

can add plenty of storage but actually claim very little space. A beautiful secretary situated in a corner can be the ideal spot for paying bills. A custom-crafted armoire or a charming painted cupboard can be outfitted for placement of a computer and printer that are out of sight once doors are shut. Even if you don't need to draw on this space for work-related activities, a Grecian sofa placed by a window or a wing chair and tea table claiming a quiet corner might be just the spot for tea and the morning paper. Traditional style is adaptable to almost every situation. You'll be pleasantly surprised at how wonderfully it falls into place once you establish your needs.

OPPOSITE: Dark wood has a more formal feeling than does light wood, thus making the former perfectly suited to this high-style dining room. Yellow walls with molded trim and a lovely fireplace with a neoclassical surround and carved paterae (the oval ornamentations in the surround) contribute to the elegance. The Oriental rug, gilt-framed landscape atop the mantel, wall sconces, and china and stemware on the table help convey traditional style.

ABOVE: The epitome of scaled-back beauty, this dining room takes its cue from the turn of the century and combines a handsome oak table and side chairs with a small case piece that acts as a buffet. Yellow walls with an attractive painted border and bare hardwood flooring allow the furnishings to take center stage. Unadorned windows provide an abundance of natural light, making the room bright and cheery.

Accessories

At last it's time to turn your attention to the myriad details that make all the difference between an impersonal space and a signature setting. You'll want your traditional dining room to say "welcome" and project solid comfort—the type of room where time can slip away unnoticed as guests converse leisurely over coffee and dessert. One suggestion is to include flowers. A beautiful bouquet of freshly cut flowers, whether on the table or mantelpiece, adds instant elegance.

Artwork can be both decorative and personal, so display favorite paintings on the walls of the dining room. Regardless of whether you're drawn to oil paintings, watercolors, or old prints, the dining room is the perfect spot to showcase them. For something a bit different, create a focal point by arranging artwork close together but hung at various heights along a single wall. This is a nice departure from the usual gallerylike arrangement.

A gilt-framed mirror is every bit as at home in the dining room as it is in the living room. Mirrors were valuable objects in the Colonial-era home and thus were given a place of prominence. The glass for early examples had to be imported from England, and frames were then made in the colonies. Tall, narrow mirrors were fashionable early on and often displayed decorative scrolled frames in a wood finish. By the mid-eighteenth century, mirror designs had expanded to include large, ornate versions with gilt frames intended for use above the mantel. Other mirrors took on architectural qualities as their gilt frames were embellished with moldings and pediments. During the early 1800s, round, convex mirrors were in vogue and these were often adorned with an eagle at the top and a classical motif at the bottom. Thereafter, mirrors were produced according to the latest fashion in interior design and have maintained their significance in the home, where they still serve as a prominent, decorative feature. While an antique version may be impossible to find or well out of financial reach, historical replicas are available at more modest costs.

Other decorative details in today's traditional dining room include the display of favorite plates on dining room walls. This embellishment was used during the Colonial era and was no doubt used in European cottages long before that. Wire plate hangers are available in a variety of styles and finishes, and you can group plates in any number of pleasing designs to serve as an accent or a focal point. Choose a single color or pattern, or an eye-catching arrangement of mismatched family heirlooms.

Finally, your table setting is more than just a mere necessity associated with fine dining. It's a personal expression—from the elegant tablecloth and handsome china to the glass or crystal and silverware. These are the patterns and designs that appeal to you. Show them off. Use them regularly. Family and friends will feel welcome and appreciate—even admire—your special attention to detail.

⋞⋟⋞⋟

OPPOSITE: Period furnishings and an assortment of collectibles make this Colonial-style dining room inviting. White walls and plank flooring are a pleasing backdrop for wooden furnishings that include a tavern table, Windsor chairs, and a large pewter cupboard. Baskets hung from wooden beams and numerous period objects on display make this a wonderful place to dine.

RIGHT, TOP: If space allows, the traditional dining room is the ideal setting for a large hutch or step-back cupboard that can be used to display favorite china or collectibles. This beautiful cupboard with weathered blue paint showcases a medley of objects including dishes, colored glassware, silver, and a small bust. The country spirit is dressed up with a pair of oval portraits and delicate matching armchairs.

RIGHT, BOTTOM: A casually elegant dining area combines a modern square table with matching Windsor chairs. The wood-beamed ceiling and low brick wall add a touch of country style. These rugged textures are tempered with floral drapes, a lovely oil landscape, and a tall bouquet of flowers.

Chapter Four

THE KITCHEN

Well over three hundred years ago, the kitchen was the center of activity in the home, and although the concept of the kitchen itself has changed over the years, this room has remained steadfast as the heart of the home.

In the single-room houses of the pre-industrial era, the massive cooking hearth was the focal point of the all-purpose "hall." As homes grew larger, interior space on the ground floor was divided to allow for a parlor, and cooking and other household chores were conducted in a separate keeping room. These early kitchens were furnished with a worktable that may also have served as a dining table. A corner cupboard housed the family's meager collection of pewter dishes and crockery, and at the hearth, an assortment of heavy iron kettles, skillets, and utensils was constantly in use.

By the late 1700s, town houses were built with basement kitchens, and in less urban areas, the kitchen often took the form of a separate cookhouse located near the main dwelling. Small homes were enlarged with a back wing to serve as a kitchen so that the keeping room could be converted into a formal parlor or, later, a dining room.

During the early to mid-1800s, little changed in regard to the kitchen. In many urban houses it became the domain of domestic servants, as middle-class wealth increased and women took on a supervisory role in the home. Furnishings such as the step-back cupboard, pie safe, and dry sink were added to accommodate the growing list of kitchen accoutrements, and the cookstove replaced hearth cooking during the 1840s and 1850s. During this time, the kitchen proper also had an adjoining pantry for keeping staples, as well as a scullery or laundry room for doing the family wash and preparing fruits and vegetables for canning. All in all, the kitchen was plain but serviceable. Walls were painted a neutral color, and floors were brick or painted wood covered with an oilcloth.

OPPOSITE: Timeless European styling has inspired a kitchen that's functional as well as beautiful. Hand-painted custom cabinetry with formal crown moldings lends architectural interest, while open shelving and a built-in plate rack put everyday objects on display. Sunny yellow tile backsplashes behind the sink and stove add brightness and color to recessed areas that would otherwise be dark.

ABOVE: Cabinetry is a focal point in any kitchen. This lovely example features a light wood finish, brass pulls, and glazed inserts in the upper cabinet doors for added architectural interest. Classic checkered flooring is given a polished look with a rich red Oriental runner. Handsome and durable granite counters salute the past. The open shelves flanking the window are perfect for displaying a collection of teapots.

The 1870s and 1880s saw the introduction of indoor plumbing and gas lines in cities, which made it more convenient to relocate the kitchen from the basement to the ground floor. The kitchen slowly began to reflect some of the decorative elements lavished on other rooms in the house. Wooden wainscoting and pressed-tin ceilings were used in the kitchen during the Victorian age because they were considered sanitary. Decorative plate rails lined the room and displayed favorite china, while the newest concept in flooring— linoleum—could be found in many middle-class kitchens. Freestanding cupboards and dressers were still used for storage, but built-in cabinets began to be incorporated in kitchen designs. A drop-leaf or gateleg table stood nearby for casual meals.

During the late nineteenth century, domestic science authorities campaigned for light and airy kitchens that would relieve some of the drudgery associated with the overwhelming list of kitchen tasks. Toward this end, windows were dressed with light curtains, walls were painted in what were referred to as "cheerful" tints (such as soft green), and a comfortable chair was recommended for a weary cook.

The emphasis in the 1890s and early 1900s on scientific processes and sanitary measures transformed the kitchen into a laboratorylike setting with crisp tile walls, tile or linoleum flooring, gleaming appliances, and porcelain sinks. Tall oak furnishings were common, and built-in cupboards with glass-front doors were practical and even a bit decorative. White and green were the favored colors for kitchen walls.

Kitchen design as we know it today, with a continuous countertop and built-in cabinets, evolved during the 1930s and 1940s. During this period (and actually up until the 1970s) the kitchen was relatively small, isolated from other rooms in the house, and considered mainly a workroom. The past few decades, however, have seen the kitchen return to the concepts of the past, and this room has emerged once again as a center of family activity. As a result, today's ideal kitchen is large enough to accommodate a number of activities, and it's as well dressed as any room in the home. It is now more "furnished" than simply outfitted with cupboards and appliances.

To create a beautiful kitchen that displays all the elements of traditional style, we call upon the materials, patterns, and colors of the past. First and foremost, however, the kitchen must be functional. Consider how much time you actually spend preparing meals, how much space you require, and the kitchen's location in relation to other areas of the home. Do activities other than cooking take place in the kitchen? Do you prefer flooring and walls that are extremely easy to maintain? Are gusts welcome in the kitchen while you're preparing a meal? After giving thought to such practical matters and planning the layout of your kitchen accordingly, you can turn your attention to the decorative aspects of kitchen design.

<><><>

ABOVE: Beautiful craftsmanship is a hallmark of Arts and Crafts style. Formal wooden cabinetry complete with crown moldings, a dark green tiled backsplash, and period light fixtures create the spirit of the style. A handsome and practical island provides convenient space for a wine rack, cookbooks, and a second kitchen sink.

ABOVE: Here's proof that the kitchen can be just as well dressed as any other room in the home. European elegance—in the molded pine cabinetry, terra-cotta tile floor, and mammoth butcher-block table—adds to this warm and inviting room. The spirit of traditional style is not the least bit compromised by the use of modern recessed lighting. For good measure, a trio of hanging fixtures with glass shades is positioned above the island housing a sink.

OPPOSITE: Beautiful custom-crafted cabinetry has the look of fine furniture. These honey pine cupboards are lavished with moldings, an elegant cornice, and large wooden pulls for a traditional European look. The work areas and floor are surfaced with tile, which is both practical and attractive. Glass-front and open cupboards showcase a collection of favorite dishes and canisters.

ABOVE: The spirit of Shaker style fills this spacious kitchen. The dark green cabinetry is simple yet beautifully designed, with vertical boards creating an appealing pattern on the doors. An open cupboard and plate rack show off colorful dishes that accent the green and white color scheme. A table that matches the counters and the checkered-pattern rattan chairs provide a place for casual family meals.

Cabinets

Since kitchen cabinets are a focal point due to their sheer presence and numbers, they can set the tone for a traditional decor. To fill your room with the spirit of the past, consider cabinets with notable architectural moldings or cornices that convey period style. Rich cherry or walnut cabinets with crown moldings and brass knobs infuse the kitchen with a formal air. For dramatic impact, cabinets can even include pilasters on cabinet corners. Glass-front cabinets in a natural wood finish will recall the high-style butler's pantry of the Victorian age and can even be given a fresh, updated look with white or pastel paint.

Custom cabinetry can be costly but well worth the investment. For those seeking a solution that's a bit more affordable, cabinets can be enhanced with decorative raised panels and select hardware for architectural flair. Porcelain or glass knobs, iron door pulls and hinges, and even simple painted knobs can be used to create varying effects.

While dark woods are usually associated with an elegant kitchen, they can also be used in a more relaxed setting. Be sure to keep in mind that a small kitchen may seem dreary if dark woods are used throughout. Oak cabinets are the first choice in an Arts and Crafts–style kitchen, and they can be made all the more beautiful with frosted or etched glass panes in cabinet doors. Maple or pine cupboards are ideal in a kitchen with old-world charm, especially when they're outfitted with white porcelain knobs.

In a casual kitchen where you desire a more relaxed decor, painted cabinets can be a cost-effective alternative that offers surprising results. The simple beauty of a Shaker-inspired kitchen can be achieved by painting cabinetry a medium blue and using plain wooden pegs as door pulls. Or a semiformal country kitchen with traditional roots might call for cabinets painted an old-time color, such as cranberry red or bayberry green. Several companies that specialize in period furniture also offer high-quality paints in colors reproducing the softness of age-old tints, which are appropriate for use on cabinets. For enhanced flavor, painted cabinets can also be stenciled with a period design.

Along with your kitchen cabinets, consider installing an island to match if the size and layout of your kitchen allow for such an added feature. An island can be both practical and decorative, and is ideal when you need something to serve as a divider between a kitchen/ dining area or a kitchen/living room.

Another desirable element in a traditional kitchen is a freestanding cupboard—for ambience as well as for practical purposes. Again, if room allows, an antique or reproduction corner cabinet, a handsome dresser, or a step-back cupboard will enhance the style of a formal or casual period room. Overhead racks for storing pots and pans will lend an authentic touch to a rustic European-style kitchen. A large French baker's rack goes hand in hand with a French Provençal decor, as does a beautiful armoire used to hide tablecloths and linens.

❧❧❧

OPPOSITE: Color is the focal point in this charming kitchen. The cabinets have been painted a bright green and accented with white pulls, while the glass cupboard doors have been lined with shirred white fabric. Artistically arranged Depression-era kitchen items on the wall-hung shelves and counter proudly proclaim this to be the home of a collector.
ABOVE: Creating a fabulous traditional-style kitchen doesn't have to break the bank. Here, cabinetry is given a new lease on life with a fresh coat of blue paint and new hinges and pulls. A casual country decorating scheme also calls for simple plank wood flooring and vintage food tins on display.

Wall Treatments

Cabinets may set the tone in your kitchen, but color will give it spirit. Is your kitchen a room unto itself, or is there an adjoining sitting area or dining space? In the kitchen that stands alone, color can be a matter of personal choice, but if you are confronted with a combination area, you'll want to consider ways to both unify and define spaces. Deep colors can have dramatic impact in the kitchen, while pastels or neutrals allow wood tones to take center stage. And white is never out of style—a white kitchen has constant classic appeal.

Paint is an obvious choice for walls in a traditional kitchen. Regardless of whether you're remodeling or just sprucing up, a fresh coat of paint gives the kitchen a new lease on life. Painted walls can become a subtle background for the well-appointed kitchen, or they can make a more obvious, bold statement. A deep hunter green has strong impact, whereas a pale sunny yellow creates an airy, sometimes playful effect. And don't forget the ceiling in the kitchen, which is usually painted white or a tint lighter than that found on the walls.

Wallpaper can be used in combination with paint as a dado or frieze, or walls can be treated to an allover wallpaper effect. With the high-quality vinyl-coated wallpapers available today, there's no reason not to use them in the kitchen. A vinyl paper is scrubbable and therefore easy to maintain. In a traditional kitchen, consider blue and white striped wallpaper for formal appeal, or a soft floral print, perhaps with a repeating geometric pattern.

A William Morris–style paper will enhance an Arts and Crafts setting, and a mini print is right at home in a traditional kitchen with country flair.

A wallpaper border can be used to design a chair rail, or you can opt to use the real thing—wooden molding—for architectural interest. Moldings can also be used as decorative cornices and baseboards. For a stronger wood statement, beadboard wainscoting can be used on kitchen walls to recall the late Victorian age. For country charm and old-world appeal, how about a stunning wood-beamed ceiling in the traditional kitchen?

⟨⟩✕⟨⟩

LEFT: This kitchen has no wall cabinets for storage, but a beautiful plate rack and a ceiling rack for pans work just as well. The paint on the woodwork has been distressed to give it a rustic look, which is continued in the worn vintage table and untreated plank floor. Personal touches give evidence of the owner's love for the great outdoors: note the duck pattern on the area rug, the fish-print window shades, and the lovely landscape above the stove.
ABOVE: Old-world charm is elevated to new heights in this kitchen, where walls are bedecked with a lovely wallpaper. The yellow background hightlights a large floral motif that's ideally suited to a large space. Gleaming copper pots and pans, and the rich wood tones of a butcher-block table and country cupboard complement the color scheme. Homey touches include the cushioned rocker, lace-edged curtains, and even the tassel tied to the key in the door.

Floor Treatments

There are several hardworking surfaces in the kitchen, the largest of which is the floor. Durability, easy maintenance, and comfort underfoot are important considerations when choosing a floor covering for the traditional-style kitchen. Fortunately, there are several easy-care options available that still afford elegant style.

Today's resilient flooring is a popular alternative to more costly ceramic tile. It is also favored for its somewhat softer surface—a plus for cooks who spend a lot of time on their feet in the kitchen. Available in a wide range of colors and patterns, resilient flooring is easy to match to a classic decorating scheme. There are designs available with the look of marble, tile, brick, or even wood flooring. Depending upon the effect you wish to create, inlaid vinyl flooring can be purchased in wide rolls (thus eliminating a lot of seams), or solid vinyl tiles can be purchased in a twelve-by-twelve-inch (30.5 by 30.5cm) size. When shopping for flooring, keep in mind that inlaid vinyl flooring (with the pattern running all the way through, surface to underside) is longer-lasting and of better quality than printed vinyl flooring, on which the pattern has been applied to the surface only.

The beauty of resilient flooring is found in the fact that you can devise any number of striking, decorative effects in the kitchen. Where a dominant color with just a hint of

RIGHT: An eye-catching patterned marble floor is a traditional accent in this stylish kitchen. Custom cabinetry with handsome moldings and a glossy blue-gray finish makes an elegant focal point and softens the modern steel table and stove hood. An aged butcher-block table serves as a miniature island on which to place finished dishes. The tools of the cook's trade are quite decorative when made of copper.

pattern is desired, you can use vinyl tiles to create a handsome border. For something a bit bolder, use patterned tiles to create the illusion of a rug in the kitchen area. You can design a geometric pattern, opt for florals, or play up stripes. Two all-time favorite flooring patterns in a traditional kitchen are a black and white checkered design and a white background with black diamonds. You can rely on these timeless classics for instant style using the black and white color scheme, or get creative and call upon blue and white or green and white. While personal style will direct you toward the colors and patterns you love, spending quality time in specialty stores will help you fully appreciate the flooring selections available.

Ceramic tile is also an ideal choice for the kitchen. As with resilient flooring, there are myriad options in regard to color, pattern, and style. Unglazed tiles are superior to glazed tiles in the kitchen if you are concerned about slippery spots due to spills. If you do install a glazed tile, look for one

OPPOSITE: Country spirit reigns supreme in this cheery kitchen. White cabinetry and light walls keep the handsome wooden flooring from making the room dark and dreary. Wrought-iron hardware adds a Colonial touch, as does the simple metal chandelier. A round table and ladder-back chairs with woven seats reinforce the country theme. Antique baskets and stoneware jars create an artful display atop the wall cabinets. RIGHT: This elegant kitchen features white cabinetry and a center island trimmed with chrome and vintage-style drawer pulls. Marble countertops, pendant hanging light fixtures, and a handsome Renaissance Revival–style sideboard placed against the far wall are decidedly Victorian touches. While the fixtures are noteworthy, striking architecture is really the star of this kitchen, from the unusual arched ceiling to the brick-lined alcove that houses the stove.

with a matte finish, which is less likely to become a hazard when wet.

In a more casual traditional kitchen, quarry tiles can be an excellent choice. Generally available in a variety of earth tones and the popular terra-cotta, quarry tiles have a more rustic look and are well suited to a country decor.

Most resilient and nonresilient (stone or tile) flooring can be maintained with damp mopping, but check the manufacturer's guidelines for instructions regarding the use of mild soaps or cleansers.

If a vinyl flooring or tile isn't your taste, perhaps you prefer the old-fashioned charm of a handsome wood floor. A traditional kitchen with either a formal or casual air can benefit from the warmth of a wood floor, provided it meets your needs. Both gleaming hardwood and parquet work well in a period setting and can be accented with an Oriental or a needlepoint rug. In a casual kitchen you may prefer something less formal, such as plank flooring that is composed of boards of random width. Yet another idea for a more casual setting is a wood floor that's been painted, stenciled, or "washed" with color for a decorative effect.

Kitchen Counters

The other hardworking surface in the kitchen is, of course, the countertop. The selection of materials used for counters includes tile, wood, granite, marble, plastic laminate, and solid plastics. Granite and marble countertops can be lovely but very expensive. On the plus side, however, they last forever and provide a wonderful surface for bakers. Either adds an authentic classic touch to a traditional kitchen. Tile is also a welcome choice, and one that allows for creative play with color and pattern to achieve truly unique designs. And don't stop at the counter—carry tiles up the wall to create a backsplash, or use them behind the stove as a decorative and protective wall covering. Tile is adaptable to any period style, from Colonial to Arts and Crafts—the secret is in the colors and patterns you choose.

A butcher block has a warm, homey look and is a nice touch in a casual kitchen with a traditional country decor. What's more, a butcher block is ideal on a kitchen island or as an insert in the counter-top area, where it's used specifically for chopping.

Plastic laminates are available today in virtually any color, and solid plastics such as Dupont Corian are more expensive but well worth the cost, given their longevity and durability. Keep in mind your color scheme when choosing a countertop material, and decide upon a pattern or design to dress up or tone down a classically styled kitchen.

Since the kitchen includes work centers, you'll want adequate lighting to ensure comfort and convenience. Most kitchens are planned with a workstation in mind, allowing for convenient placement of the stove, refrigerator, and sink. The result is usually a kitchen designed in an L-shape, a U-shape, or, in a smaller kitchen, a galley or corridor. The workstation is where you need to concentrate task lighting, while general lighting can serve as a secondary light source.

For countertop and cooking areas, consider installing recessed lighting, which is highly functional without being obtrusive. In a traditional decor, the hidden nature of recessed lighting is a distinct advantage—the state-of-the-art, high-tech features are concealed from view and therefore won't detract from the age-old appeal of a classic kitchen. In contrast, and for an obvious period look, pendant lights (available in any number of styles) can be hung in strategic positions about the work area.

Lighting

General lighting in the traditional kitchen can take the form of a handsome ceiling fixture, a pendant light, or even a chandelier positioned above the kitchen table or center island. Antique reproductions are available in a variety of styles, colors, and designs. A kitchen with Colonial ambience would be the perfect spot for a chandelier with iron arms that curve out and up. For a Victorian-period theme, pendant lamps with colored glass or art glass shades contribute an authentic touch.

Finally, what about track lighting? By all means, unless you reside in a living history museum, go ahead and take advantage of the general lighting provided by these contemporary fixtures. While at first thought they may seem terribly out of place in a traditional decor, you are, after all, creating an impression of style—not a literal rendition. Besides, track lighting tends to blend into the background—especially if white track lighting is used against a white ceiling.

❧❦❧

OPPOSITE: The natural materials found in the wooden cabinetry and terra-cotta floor of this kitchen evoke the spirit of the past. A traditional ceramic sink contributes an English country mood. Note, too, how windows without a treatment can be beautiful, especially when their handsome sills and sashes frame a pleasant view.

LEFT: The difference is always in the details. Uncurtained windows allow the cooks a wonderful view, while the sills and sashes display a bouquet of daisies in a silver mug, a beautiful blue glass bowl, and ripening fruit. Green-gray cabinetry is paired with a light gray marble counter and backsplash to create an understated elegance in this sunny kitchen.

BELOW: Simple touches can often have a big impact. Elegant swags in a traditional blue and white striped fabric make a stylistic statement and add charm to this small kitchen. A neutral tile backsplash, a window box of fresh herbs, and transparent glass jars break up the whiteness of the walls and cabinetry.

Windows and window dressings can be used to achieve amazing results in a traditional kitchen. Situating a window over the sink is ideal, as it will provide good lighting for dishwashing and a pleasant view to make a dull task more interesting. By adding a beautiful Palladian window you can create the illusion of architectural history and classic style. French doors will open a kitchen to the outdoors and provide easy access to a patio nearby. Windows with decorative moldings also lend old-world charm, as do multipaned windows with transoms.

Dress windows with curtains made of cotton, linen, muslin, lace, sheers, or chintz. Use decorative rods for a formal look, or choose wooden dowels for a country-style room. Coordinating the fabric used at the windows with any upholstery in the kitchen creates a polished look. And where a curtain isn't necessarily called for, leave the window bare or consider a valance, swag and jabot, or light-filtering shade.

Furnishings

A great many kitchens have enough space for a table and chairs or have an adjoining breakfast nook or dining area to accommodate these pieces. With this in mind, you'll want to add furnishings that heighten your traditional style. Even though the kitchen is a highly functional space, that doesn't mean it can't be gracious as well. A trestle table or gateleg table accompanied by Windsor or Chippendale-style chairs can add Colonial spirit to a kitchen and convey the warmth of this period style. For a subtle French influence, a long oak harvest table with rush-seat chairs creates a European ambience. If something a bit more dressy is called for, add patterned chair cushions and a beautiful woven table runner. A round table bedecked with an embroidered linen tablecloth can play host to neoclassical side chairs for a delicate but stately look. Or place upholstered slipper chairs, wicker seating, or fabric-covered balloon-back chairs around the same round table for a Victorian feel.

A round oak table with pressed-back chairs can be adapted to fit either a casual country-style kitchen or one with a more formal Victorian decor. Oak is also the perfect choice in an Arts and Crafts–style kitchen, where plain and simple make a strong but elegant statement. Even something as modern as a glass-top table can have amazing decorative power when juxtaposed with period chairs in a traditional setting. Remember that seating in the kitchen doesn't always have to be a matched set: assorted chairs of a similar style and size can be grouped around the table in a casual kitchen with pleasing results.

ABOVE: Warm, golden pine infuses this room with English country style. The step-back cupboard is filled with a jumble of mismatched dishes in beautiful colors and patterns, which enhances the old-world charm. More of a great room than a traditional kitchen, this space can accommodate a dining table and chairs as well as the usual kitchen fixtures.
OPPOSITE: A vintage-style cookstove is the star of this country kitchen. Wooden flooring and a brick wall combine to make a rustic backdrop for an assortment of kitchen collectibles that includes enamelware, china canisters, and earthenware jars. Favorite items on display add a personal touch that gives this cozy kitchen a one-of-a-kind spirit.

RIGHT: A wall treatment of white bead-board reveals this kitchen's Victorian roots, but the Depression-era stove and stylish teapot give the space a modern flair. Above the gleaming white stove, shelves hold spices and other cooking necessities. Cups placed on hooks provide bold dashes of color, while the framed photographs of a bulldog add a sense of whimsy.

Accessories

To really make the kitchen the heart of your home, you'll want to personalize it with decorative accessories, antiques and collectibles, and favorite kitchen-related items. Decorative touches can be as simple as clay pots filled with herbs lined up on a sunny window ledge or as elegant as brass fixtures for the kitchen sink.

To show off beautiful copper cookware, suspend an overhead rack above the stove or center island and fill it with pots, pans, and utensils. To keep recipe books handy but out of the way, incorporate open shelving into kitchen cabinets. The same can be done for wine bottles, and a built-in wine rack can add a decorative measure that equals its practical purpose. These little attentions to detail give a traditional kitchen a finished look.

The kitchen with old-world charm can serve as a wonderful display case for cherished collectibles. Obviously a vintage dresser or hutch can be filled with pottery, dishes, baskets, or glass jars, but so can the space between cabinet tops and the ceiling, as well as out-of-the-way countertop areas. A plate rail running around the perimeter of the room is ideal for beautiful dishes, or a collection of plates can be grouped on a wall.

Personalize your kitchen with artwork you admire. A collection of prints or a singular painting can have an elegant impact in a formal setting. Artistic merit can also be found underfoot with a decorative needlepoint area rug, or even atop the table with a tapestry runner. In a traditional kitchen with country flair, a vintage quilt can be used as a table dressing, but be sure to protect it with a glass top.

Think fruit and flowers in the traditional kitchen. A beautiful pottery bowl filled with apples and pears or lemons and limes can become a still-life focal point. Flowers are welcome in any kitchen, no matter what your personal style. Add these and other details to complete your period decor. You'll have a kitchen that will serve you well and wrap you in the warmth of home for hour after pleasurable hour.

ABOVE: When it comes to decorative accessories in the kitchen, nothing speaks of traditional style like gleaming copper cookware. Here, a metal rack keeps a beautiful assortment of pots and pans out of the way but easily within reach. A large wood-topped island complete with a sink provides plenty of work space. The professional-quality stove is set into an alcove defined by formal architectural detailing.

Chapter Five
THE FAMILY ROOM

The concept of a living space devoted to family activities has been a part of home design for centuries. During the pre-industrial era, when space was at a premium, the all-purpose hall, and then later the keeping room, were designated areas for family work as well as family fun. As architectural designs became more elaborate and rooms were planned according to specific functions, the Victorian-era sitting room became the family's cozy retreat. This nineteenth-century version of the family room was a private space rather than a public area used for social entertaining. The sitting room was often located on the first floor of the home, behind the formal parlor, although sometimes the sitting room was upstairs, along with bedrooms or chambers.

The nineteenth-century sitting room was feminine in appearance. Cast-off furnishings from the parlor were given a fresh look with flowery chintz fabrics, and an upholstered easy chair or chaise longue was added for solid comfort. The sitting room might contain bookcases full of the latest publications or a musical instrument, such as a piano or organ, for celebratory sing-alongs. The mistress of the house usually kept her work basket in the sitting room so that she could retreat to a quiet corner and a comfy chair to do a bit of needlework. A small center table or card table was usually included among the furnishings, so that the family could play card games and board games.

The sitting room almost mirrored the formal parlor in that the wall treatments, window dressings, and floor coverings used would be thought fussy by today's standards. Upon looking more closely, however, one would see that the furniture was not of the latest fashion, the walls were painted or papered but not terribly elaborate, windows were dressed with fabrics more practical than decorative, and the carpet was an inexpensive version that would wear well. This was a casual and relaxed setting for the Victorians.

OPPOSITE: Stately columns accentuate the high ceilings of this light, spacious family room. Fabric patterns are juxtaposed with pleasing results, giving the setting a polished look. The vibrant area rugs anchor the room while still showing off a beautiful wood floor.
ABOVE: Dark walls can turn the family room into everyone's favorite retreat. Deep green is the perfect choice for a traditional effect, especially when paired with a sumptuous red leather sofa. Piled high with kilim pillows, the sofa is the ideal spot to read, and a casual wooden coffee table keeps favorite books close at hand. The couch is so beloved that a portrait of it hangs on the wall.

ABOVE: The family room, a designated place to relax, should speak of casual comfort. In this example, cheery yellow and white striped walls provide a pleasing backdrop for a plump love seat with a floral print and two open armchairs. By introducing favorite artwork, a couple stacks of books, comfy pillows, and a checkered throw, the owner has created a space with the ultimate in creature comforts.

First consider the purpose your family room will serve. Is it going to function as an entertainment center, complete with a television, a VCR, and stereo equipment? Or is it for quieter pursuits, such as reading and conversation? Will you need space for a work area, such as a handsome desk? If your family room is open to the kitchen, will it incorporate a table and chairs for casual family meals? What will serve as the focus of the family room: a fireplace, built-in bookshelves, or perhaps a lovely view of the great outdoors? And finally, do you want your family room to convey casual elegance or a "put your feet up on the coffee table" air?

Wall Treatments

Once you decide how the family room can best suit your lifestyle, you can give serious thought to decorating the space to meet your needs. The traditional family room that's actually a separate space can take on the look of a polished den or a stately library with paneled walls. A dark paneling will give the room a handsome, rich look, while a lighter wood or whitewashed boards used as paneling will create a country effect. Salvaged or recycled boards or paneling can be used for authentic Colonial appeal or for a more rustic charm. Architectural salvage is a booming business today, and large warehouses as well as smaller workshops can be found almost everywhere. Their inventories are inspiring, and while you may pay a visit in search of vintage lumber, you'll no doubt walk away with several ideas for incorporating other salvaged goods into the family room and the rest of the house as well.

For a lighter, more spacious look, walls in the family room can be painted. A warm, dark color will enhance the feeling that the family room is a cozy retreat, especially when combined with an inviting fireplace and comfortable seating. Light colors, on the other hand, can brighten a small space considerably, and prove ideal in a setting that doubles as a work area. Paint walls some variation of white and choose pewter or Colonial red for trim in a family room reminiscent of an old-fashioned keeping room. Pastels are perfect when joined with crisp wicker furnishings to give a suggestion of the outdoors moved inside. Even bold primary colors can

As the elaborate rituals and customs of nineteenth-century culture faded away, more simplified lifestyles took hold and homes began to reflect the move toward more casual living and entertaining. Bungalows were built with open living spaces that reflected informal activities, but it wasn't until the massive move to the suburbs in the 1950s that the family room became a common feature in home design. Call it what you will—the den, the great room, or simply the family room—but many of today's homes include a relaxed, laid-back space for rest, relaxation, and home-based activities.

Regardless of whether your family room is an open space adjacent to the kitchen or a cozy room unto itself, casual comfort should be the theme. Traditional home design will accomplish this with style, subtle elegance, and a timeless beauty that can be both playful and practical.

be a playful addition to the family room that sports a relaxed, traditional country decorating scheme.

Wallpaper, too, can be used in the family room with amazing results, and the possibilities with wallpaper are endless. Stripes, geometrics, and florals are versatile enough that they can be used in both formal and casual rooms, and these, along with other patterns, are available in a wide array of colors. Keep in mind that you can always match upholstery with a wallpaper pattern for a coordinated look in a more classic family room.

For a departure from the traditional stripes that have long been favored as a wallpaper treatment, you can always consider a delicate mini print in the traditional family room that calls to mind a country cottage or scaled-down country decorating theme. Trompe l'oeil wallpapers can be used for fun; consider a "fool the eye" pattern that one would swear was actually a wall of bookcases filled with books. If anything Oriental is your passion, how about an exotic grass cloth wall covering in a traditional family room that's home to bamboo furnishings, Chinese porcelain, and potted palms? Or you can choose a wallpaper pattern in a warm hue, such as deep red, and accessorize it with rich greens, soft pinks, and cream-colored accents for a truly relaxed setting that's as lovely as it is comfortable and inviting.

Other considerations come into play when the family room is an extended living space off the kitchen. Naturally, you'll want one space to flow into the next, and yet each should have its own signature marks at the same time. Actually, this type of arrangement offers wonderful possibilities in regard to wall treatments. The open expanse of a combination kitchen/family room might have a beautiful tongue-and-groove vaulted ceiling or a beamed ceiling that imparts instant casual charm. Walls can be painted white to unify such a space and allow the ceiling to take center stage. A wall of windows or French doors that open onto a terrace or

LEFT: A deep color can make a large room appear more intimate and inviting. This family room features red walls accented with white trim. Floral, striped, and checkered fabrics happily coexist on furnishings that include a plump sofa, easy chairs, and a round, fringed ottoman placed before the hearth. A medley of favorite accessories, from topiaries and gilt-framed paintings to books and majolica plates, personalize this family space.

OPPOSITE: Traditional country style makes for relaxed living in this spacious setting. The medley of family room furnishings includes a beautiful Shaker rocker with a signature tape seat, a wicker armchair, and a tailored sofa. A wooden trunk makes an ideal casual coffee table, and a lovely area rug with a geometric and floral motif defines the sitting area before the brick hearth.

ABOVE: Colonial ambience makes for a warm and inviting family room. The glossy wooden flooring, paneled red fireplace wall, and stenciled border on the white wall enhance the period theme. A camel-back sofa, a comfy wing chair, and Windsor chairs are gathered around the hearth to create a cozy sitting area. A reproduction tin chandelier, wall sconces, and a pie safe filled with collectible china are the perfect accessories.

patio can serve as an instant focal point that allows Mother Nature the spotlight, complemented by soft, nature-inspired hues in the rest of the room. Neutral colors and pastels are also excellent choices in a family room that extends off the kitchen. Wallpaper can be used to add a decorative or dramatic touch in such a floor plan. A wallpaper border used as a chair rail or frieze will unify an open family room when wallpaper has also been used in the kitchen. This not only serves to lend a coordinated look to your decorating scheme, but it extends your "style" from the kitchen to the family room and creates a sense of flow and continuity between the two spaces.

Floor Treatments

Flooring in the traditional family room should be practical and functional as well as beautiful. If the room is a separate space, wall-to-wall carpeting is an obvious choice for comfort and convenience. Since children and pets usually have free rein in the family room and there's generally a great deal of traffic in and out of this popular spot, carpeting should be durable. Among the many options, consider a textured carpet, a Berber, or a cut and loop for a casual setting. A textured carpet is soil-resistant, won't show footprints, and can easily be "dressed" by placing a favorite area rug atop it. Berber carpets have a tweed look to them and are long-wearing. A cut and loop is easily recognized by its sculptured pattern, which is not only decorative but practical in that it tends to wear evenly and doesn't show dirt or stains. All of the above types are available in a vast selection of colors to suit a traditional decorating scheme.

If carpet just won't do and you'd like something either a bit more refined or more relaxed, consider a wood floor. A handsome hardwood floor can add a touch of elegance to a casual traditional room. By adding a beautiful Oriental rug, a needlepoint rug, or sisal matting, you instantly elevate the refined, decorative effect of the floor and can designate seating or conversation areas at the same time. A wood floor in the family room can also convey a more rustic feeling by using wide planks rather than narrow boards, while a spirited air is conveyed when a wood floor is painted or decorated using special techniques such as stenciling or spattering.

Ceramic tiles are another popular flooring treatment in the traditional family room, especially when the room extends off the kitchen. Ceramic tiles are long-wearing and easy to maintain (see chapter 4 for more information on tiles). They can be casual or dressy when arranged in artistic patterns. Tiles that imitate marble can be used with classical furnishings for a stately touch, or you can opt for a checkered pattern, long favored in a traditional decor. The myriad colors available make tiles suitable for any family room with traditional styling, and like hardwood floors, they can be dressed with area rugs or sisal matting for added comfort.

Brick makes an excellent flooring choice in the family room that also serves as a conservatory. The rustic good looks and durability of brick complement the casual nature of an indoor setting with outdoor appeal. When set in a classic pattern, such as a herringbone or chevron, brick can even bring a touch of elegance to the family room.

ABOVE: Elaborate architectural details—pilasters styled after Ionic columns, a beamed ceiling, and a bank of windows with a notable cornice—create a room that is both classic and contemporary. Hardwood flooring adds warmth to this minimalist setting, which is furnished with a streamlined rocker and a luxurious cushioned window seat that runs along three sides of the windowed alcove.

ABOVE: This expansive family room seems even larger than it is, thanks to the vaulted ceiling. Part home office, part living room, and even part spa (note the bathtub built into the alcove), this space meets the owner's every need. A handsome wooden desk and bookshelf are joined by contemporary furnishings, including a couch done in a classic blue and white stripe. Glass blocks set into the floor and tub surround add to the lightness of the space.

Lighting

Lighting in the traditional family room is similar to the lighting used in the living room: task, accent, and general lighting are all called into play. Given the casual, comfortable nature of the family room, save the crystal chandelier for more formal spaces and instead choose lighting fixtures that convey timeless appeal without becoming a focal point.

For task lighting, consider a brass pharmacy (pole) lamp or a reading lamp—which is adjustable and adaptable to a casual traditional decor—placed next to a favorite comfortable chair. For tabletops, a classic shape such as the ginger-jar lamp, urn lamp, or candlestick lamp can be used with a playful or creative twist. Have a lamp shade custom-crafted to match the upholstery fabric, or consider using fabric shades with a floral pattern to accompany checkered furniture fabrics—or vice versa. White lamp shades are always appealing, but a colored shade will instantly transform the feel of your room. Yellow or rose shades contribute warmth and coziness, while black shades offer classic good looks and elegant beauty.

Accent lighting in the form of wall sconces can add subtle style to the traditional family room. Brass or glass examples are ideal in a room with a touch of elegance, as are miniature candlestick lamps. Again, play up the fabric shades. Place the sconces beside an overmantel, flanking artwork, or simply in a spot where they can light and dress up a wall.

For general lighting in the family room, recessed fixtures are a wonderful idea in a relaxed setting. If you prefer something a bit more obvious and decorative, go with a hanging fixture. Whether you prefer a simple glass globe or a wrought-iron chandelier, there are numerous styles available, from rustic and Colonial to classic, Victorian, and Arts and Crafts. Spending some time in a specialty lighting store will help you fully appreciate the many available options and their decorative benefits.

ABOVE: This inviting family room takes its decorative cue from the Victorian era. A simple but lovely background of off-white walls and tile flooring showcases an antique wicker settee lavished with pillows and a vintage table surrounded by a mix of chairs. A cushioned window seat provides an ideal spot to enjoy the view. Decorative accessories are limited to an ornate metal chandelier, a favorite piece of artwork, baskets of dried flowers, and a pitcher filled with roses. OPPOSITE: Simple, elegant beauty is the end result when pine plank flooring and crisp white walls set the stage for a pair of traditional sofas dressed in striped fabric, mismatched coffee tables, and an antique wicker chair. Sisal matting used as a room-size rug lends a casual air, and carefully chosen accessories accentuate the room's timeless appeal.

Window Treatments

Window dressings in the all-purpose family room are typically less formal than those in the living or dining room. Since the family room is a relatively new concept in home design, the intention is to recreate the spirit of traditional style via time-honored furnishings, colors, and materials. With this in mind, the windows in a room devoted to comfort and ease should be low-maintenance and informal. Many times, in fact, a handsome window can be left bare if it affords a pleasing view, and if privacy is not a concern.

For windows where a dressing is required, simple tab curtains on a handsome rod are an understated way of adding beauty to your room. Used with a wooden rod, tab cur-

tains are especially at home in a Colonial-period setting. Simple pleated draw curtains, with or without a valance, are another possibility for a traditional family room, as are lightweight draperies sewn to wooden or metal café rings. Cotton, linen, dobby, muslin, and homespun tweed are good choices for draperies in a casual setting, as are durable cotton or linen blends that include acrylic or polyester, which are easy to care for and wrinkle-resistant.

Fabric shades are a nice alternative to draperies, and they lend a crisp, tailored look to the traditional family room. Color and pattern can be added to the room with minimum yardage, and Roman shades are perfect for a classic look. Depending upon the fabric you choose, a Roman shade can filter or block out light and afford privacy with a lighter touch than a full drapery treatment.

Wooden shutters are another practical and pleasing window treatment in a no-fuss room. Plantation-style shutters with louvers control lighting,

and depending upon how they're painted, they can blend in with the window frame and walls or take a more dramatic stance. Shutters also contribute subtle architectural interest. Easy to maintain, they can be dressed with a lovely fabric valance for added impact. Another possibility is horizontal blinds, which are a contemporary touch that juxtapose nicely with traditional furnishings, thanks to their straightforward design. Fabric, vinyl, and metal blinds, as well as mini blinds, are available in virtually any color to suit any decor.

❧❀❧

ABOVE: This gracious family room features a bright, spirited color scheme. Yellow walls and neutral carpeting play host to a striped sofa and color-coordinated wing chairs. Elegant swags at the windows repeat the predominant colors in an attractive floral pattern. The handsome armoire can be used for storage or for hiding home electronics, and a beautifully carved trunk acts as a coffee table.

ABOVE: This elegant family room has a formal but comfortable appeal, courtesy of the handsome dark wooden furnishings and a striking wing chair. White walls and a creamy area rug allow furnishings to stand out and prevent the room from becoming too dark. Salmon-colored draw draperies provide a traditional window dressing, and select accessories—books, flowers, and candlesticks—reinforce the classic theme. Note how the beautiful piece of artwork creates an optical illusion that makes the room seem larger.

Furnishings

When it comes to furnishing the traditional family room, comfort is paramount. This is the setting for a sink-down couch and plump, overstuffed chairs. Easy-care fabrics or slipcovers will extend a relaxed tone. Even classic styles, such as the camel-back sofa, can be dressed as if for play: juxtapose the traditional lines of the piece with a spirited checkered or striped fabric. Checks and stripes, along with ginghams and tartan plaids, are perfect for the family room, where they convey a period look. And rather than dressing the living room sofa and easy chair with a fringed or tailored skirt, how about using decorative piping in an accent color for detailing?

Other fabrics at home in the relaxed family room include French Provençal prints and cotton chintz. The multicolored fabrics of Provence feature paisley, floral, and geometric patterns in bold colors inspired by the European countryside. Combine a sofa and an easy chair decked out in a Provençal print with a few ladder-back chairs that have rush seats, and your family room instantly acquires old-world charm.

You don't have to forsake comfort for good looks when creating a family room reminiscent of the Victorian era. Flowery chintz fabric goes a long way toward conveying the spirit of the style, and throw pillows, a shawl or crazy quilt draped over the sofa, and a wicker rocking chair or two will enhance the nineteenth-century appeal.

For an Arts and Crafts–inspired family room, include a set of handsome Mission oak chairs in the room, and outfit them with leather cushions or cushions covered with a stylized William Morris print. A library or coffee table constructed in the same enduring and simplified style will reinforce the Arts and Crafts theme and serve as a lovely testament to the beauty and fine craftsmanship of this style.

While a comfortable sofa and easy chairs are a must, the traditional family room needs to meet numerous other demands as well. For example, what can be done with the television and other assorted electronics? A beautiful cupboard is often the solution to what some consider a real dilemma. However, vintage armoires, step-back cupboards, chests, or large dressers should

OPPOSITE: This warm, wood-beamed room salutes the Arts and Crafts movement. Dark wooden paneling is topped with William Morris–style wallpaper, and the fireplace surround is made of art tiles in earthy hues. An upholstered sofa and easy chairs sporting fringed skirts add a contemporary note and keep the room from feeling somber.
RIGHT: Reminiscent of a Colonial keeping room, this cozy setting includes matching wing chairs and a table brightened with a coat of green milk paint. A colorful braided rug contributes to this rustic interpretation of the period style, as do the baskets hung from the beamed ceiling and the pottery displayed in the open corner cupboard.

traditional family room. For the room that takes its cue from country style, a rustic painted bench can sit before the sofa. Or perhaps a vintage trunk or an old oak table cut down to coffee table height would be ideal.

A more refined and polished look can be achieved by pulling an ottoman up to the couch and accessorizing it with a lovely tray to steady drinks and snacks. Save the ottoman with the tailored skirt for the living room, and choose instead a handsome example with carved feet and playful upholstery.

For a period look, a pair of tea tables can be placed side by side before the sofa—perhaps you can find examples crafted by a rural cabinetmaker that display the essence of a period style in a more simplified way. Likewise, a classical setting can make use of vintage urns or a handsome piece of architectural salvage outfitted with a glass top to serve as a novel and stately coffee table.

Other furnishings, too, may be called for in the traditional family room. A long harvest table can do nicely as a worktable for hobbyists, or a desk might be required to accommodate the family computer and assorted paperwork. A striking bookcase or a wall of built-in shelves would be ideal, not only for storing books and games but also for displaying favorite collectibles and treasured family photos.

not be altered considerably to function as state-of-the-art entertainment centers because of the value of antique pieces. A more desirable alternative would be to invest in a reproduction built specifically for this purpose. Peruse any top-notch home furnishing center and you'll be amazed at the innovative choices available in regard to wall units and sizable cupboards that combine beauty with function and practicality. From the Chippendale chest-on-chest and lacquered cupboards of Oriental design to hand-painted cupboards and open-shelving systems complete with traditional moldings, there's a perfect cabinet out there to house your television with style.

Where can you put your feet up? Why, on the coffee table, of course. And the coffee table can take several different forms in a casual, relaxed

Accessories

To complete the traditional family room, consider the decorative accessories you'll want to use. This is the perfect space in which to express yourself by allowing your favorite collections and keepsakes to take center stage. Whether your passion is stoneware, vintage textiles such as quilts or samplers, art pottery, toys, folk art, wood carvings, Shaker boxes, or nautical items, let the pieces come to life in the family room. Surround yourself with cherished family photographs and favorite artwork. Add a bouquet or two of dried flowers as well as fresh flowers in season. Have afghans at the ready for curling up, and toss pillows galore to maximize comfort. Then bring the family together and enjoy.

᪐

OPPOSITE: The traditional family room may also include a home office or, at the very least, a place to tame paperwork, write letters, and pay bills. This elegant Victorian desk provides space for mail and books, as well as small drawers for stationery. A beautiful pink amaryllis housed in a casual wicker basket adds a light, casual touch to this corner.

ABOVE: A large green cupboard filled with miniature furnishings creates an instant focal point in this family room, but what's more important is that the collection personalizes the space. A grouping of wicker armchairs with red floral cushions and a matching ottoman are arranged for conversation or a spirited game of checkers. A skylight and unadorned French doors allow in plenty of light, which makes the relatively small room feel airy and spacious.

RIGHT: High-tech electronics are a fact of life, but they don't have to be the focal point in the family room. Rather, a beautiful cupboard, such as this armoire, can be used to store the television, VCR, and stereo equipment. In this way, family members can enjoy all the modern conveniences without compromising their traditional decorating style.

THE BEDROOM

The bedroom, or at the very least the master bedroom, has long been treasured in the home. Early housing was constructed with one sizable room—the hall—and beds were as common a fixture there as the spinning wheel or the worktable. By the eighteenth century, however, homes had been enlarged or constructed to accommodate a separate sleeping parlor (master bedroom) on the ground floor and additional space for sleeping quarters in an upstairs loft or attic.

The bed was an elaborate furnishing in the eighteenth-century sleeping parlor. In both England and France, the upper class had what was called a ceremonial bed, which served as a status symbol of sorts. This special piece was lavished with costly fabrics and decorated with ornamental carvings. This tradition was carried on to a lesser degree in the early North American home, where initially straw-filled mattresses and later feather mattresses were used. The tall four-poster bed was dressed with a canopy and curtains, which kept drafts at bay during the night and also allowed some measure of privacy in rooms where there might be more than one bed. Woolen fabrics

and cotton chintz in bold, bright colors and patterns were used in fashioning these early bed curtains. Checkered patterns were highly favored, as were scenic prints. For the bed itself, women spent hour upon hour creating and caring for crisp white linens, which were safely stored away in trunks or chests filled with sachets designed to lend a subtle, pleasing scent.

The highly dressed bed continued to be both practical and fashionable well into the nineteenth century, and bed curtains became more ornate with the passing of time. In the homes of the well-to-do, the bed draperies were often made of handsome white linens or silk in addition to the chintz scenic patterns and floral designs that were still in vogue.

Changing furniture styles and the advice offered by household experts that sleeping chambers should have a supply of fresh air at night contributed to the demise of bed curtains. Many such experts had long campaigned that bed curtains were a health threat as well as a fire hazard, and by the 1850s, if draperies were used at all, they were in the form of a purely decorative half-canopy with curtains arranged in a festoon near the head of the bed.

OPPOSITE: A canopy bed can be left unadorned or dressed in several ways. This elegant example features a lovely scalloped canopy with a decorative crown molding and curtains tied back at the head of the bed. The impression is one of timeless beauty, and by limiting the quantity of bed curtains, the room maintains an open and airy feeling.

ABOVE: A striking veneered chest and stately four-poster bed give this small bedroom a sense of grandeur. Striped wallpaper and gilt-framed artwork contribute to the formal feeling, while the varied patterns and colors in the bedding soften the style and add comfort.

Most bedrooms or chambers also included a wing chair or comfortable easy chair that could be placed near the warmth of the hearth.

Toward the end of the nineteenth century, sanitary measures were a key household concern, and bedrooms were often transformed into sparse settings with only the basic requirements. Heavy, carved bedsteads were replaced by painted iron or brass beds; carpeting was removed and area rugs were used; and window and bed dressings displayed a new lightness and delicacy. This theme persisted in the Arts and Crafts movement, but a handsome and simple oak bed may well have replaced a metal example. The bed, however, remained the center of attention in this room given over to rest and repose, and the same can be said today. The bed remains the focus of inventive decorative effects.

For today's traditional-style bedroom there are myriad options for interior design. There are also some elements common to all bedrooms, no matter how big or small. You'll want to keep in mind that the bed is indeed the focal point. Then think about your storage needs. Is there enough closet space? If not, consider a beautiful armoire to pick up the slack. How about chests and dressers? Are built-ins an option? For maximum comfort, is there room for an easy chair in which to simply relax? Do you watch television or read in the bedroom? What type of ambience should the room's background convey? Such concerns should be given thought before you outfit and decorate your traditional bedroom.

Naturally, this early version of interior design required that the window curtains match the bed curtains.

By this time architectural styles had resulted in homes being built with bedchambers located on the second floor of the home, and the sleeping parlor had become the formal parlor given over to entertaining and socializing sans bed. The French-inspired neoclassical sleigh bed had become popular, followed by the various Victorian styles with massive ornamental headboards and footboards.

During the Victorian age, the bedroom itself was supposed to be light and airy to promote well-being and reduce the ever-present threat of germs. Some bedrooms were light, but others were almost baronial with their dark and somber colors, layered window dressings, and carpeted floors. The Victorian advice givers persisted, however, and strongly recommended that bedroom walls be painted a pale hue and floors be covered with area rugs or sisal matting for ease in cleaning. A dressing table, a washstand, and assorted chests and bureaus were typical furnishings in a bedroom, and by the middle of the nineteenth century matching bedroom "suites" were available.

⟨⟩⟨⟩

ABOVE: A careful blend of pastel colors and pleasing patterns makes this bedroom a glorious feminine retreat. The floral carpet and matching spread and curtains lend unity. The soft green skirt that dresses the round table is coordinated with the trim on the curtains. For a casual touch, the Victorian settee is upholstered in a spirited green and white check. OPPOSITE: Simple, smart styling gives this cozy bedroom a truly signature touch. Buttery yellow walls and unadorned windows make a cheery backdrop for a bed with a headboard reminiscent of a picket fence. This fence design is repeated in the whimsical planter atop the dresser, and the garden theme is reinforced with lush flowering plants. A lovely corner cupboard answers the need for storage and display space, while a gilt-framed flower print graces the wall beside the bed.

⬖⬗⬖

LEFT: What to do when the bedroom is short on architectural flair? Simply add your own. Rather than using a formal headboard, this bed is set against a wall incorporating a display shelf and whimsical columns that have been painted on the wall. Note the clever use of the same design on the bedspread. A Chippendale chair sits proudly beside the bed, a truly traditional element in this "neoclassical" room.
OPPOSITE: A serene four-poster bed fits perfectly into this vaulted alcove. Striped wallpaper, used in tandem with white wainscoting, softens the quirky angles of the under-the-eaves bedroom. Furnishings include an antique trunk that provides storage and mismatched bedside tables that give this traditional bedroom charming personality.

Wall Treatments

First and foremost, what mood shall your bedroom walls convey? The traditional bedroom is typically painted or papered in cool colors that enhance the relaxing and restful qualities of the room. Such colors as pale blue, soft green, light lavender, and gray are serene and easy on the eyes.

Perhaps you want something a bit more lively, especially if the bedroom is situated with a northern exposure. A creamy yellow, a peach, or a pastel pink might be just the answer. For an elegant touch, consider neutral hues such as beige or taupe. Finish the room off by painting the ceiling and woodwork an elegant white. Whatever color scheme you decide upon, please yourself. After all, this is your own personal sanctuary.

Paint is by far the easiest way to decorate your walls. If, however, you can't resist having a pattern, wallpaper will certainly be more to your liking. For the bedroom that will please him as well as her, a striped pattern is an excellent compromise—lovely and traditional but not too fussy or feminine. You can always add floral bed linens for a soft touch. A mini print used in tandem with a coordinating wallpaper border is another option that works well in either a stately or a relaxed bedroom. Dress it up with coordinating fabrics on the bed, at the windows, or on a comfy wing chair. For classic appeal, select a wallpaper that sports a traditional motif, such as vase or urn shapes, trailing vines, shells, or acanthus leaves. Large floral designs and toiles de Jouy with pictorial scenes are a wonderful idea in a period setting that hints at Colonial roots. Other period styles, including Victorian and Arts and Crafts, can be achieved by choosing wallpaper that reflects the colors and designs associated the desired particular era. Keep in mind that wallpaper goes a long way in creating a finished look, especially in an under-the-eaves or attic bedroom with a slanted ceiling and odd nooks and crannies.

Fabric can also be used as a wall treatment in the traditional bedroom, and may prove ideal in older homes where walls are in less-than-perfect condition. Unless you're quite handy and long on patience, this is something best left to a professional.

⬦⬥⬦

OPPOSITE: While paint can work wonders in creating a beautiful and inviting bedroom, wallpaper is often the treatment of choice for expressing timeless appeal. The wallpaper in this bedroom appears hand-painted, and the nature-inspired motif provides a pleasing backdrop for twin four-poster beds and a cozy conversation area. Luxurious bedding in shades of yellow and a vibrant Oriental rug add vivid color and elegance.

ABOVE: This beguiling nursery is made even more attractive with an understated floral wallpaper, coordinated draperies, and wood flooring dressed with an oval needlepoint rug. A white crib with a ruffled half-circle coronet imparts traditional style, as does a venerable rocking chair. The dollhouse perched on the window ledge and the child's table and chair set are enchanting additions.

ABOVE: A curved bank of windows creates the ideal place to relax in this inviting bedroom sitting area. A traditional blue and white striped wallpaper is complemented by floral curtains and the pansy-print throw pillows on the plump, yellow easy chairs. An elegant wooden table provides a resting spot for books, flowers, and a lamp, while the tailored ottoman proves handy for serving a cozy breakfast.

Floor Treatments

You'll want either softness underfoot or the striking good looks of a wood floor accessorized with beautiful area rugs to complement your bedroom decor. Wall-to-wall carpeting helps reduce sound and can be a luxurious addition. A saxony or plush carpet provides solid comfort and long-lasting beauty, and is well suited to the master bedroom. Either is available in virtually any color and can be used as a bold or subtle decorative element. A rich, dark color, such as forest green or deep blue, will add visual interest, while a soft, pale hue can serve as a subdued background to other details throughout the room.

A wood floor can be used to create different period effects in the bedroom. Hardwood and parquet flooring bespeak elegance and gracious charm. Outfitted with a notable Oriental, French Aubusson, or needlepoint rug, the timeless beauty of a traditional-style wood floor commands attention. Consider an area rug with a geometric design in a classic decor, and use florals to convey period design from the Victoria era. In contrast, a more casual approach includes painting and/or stenciling a wood floor in a traditional country style and then using painted sisal, hooked, or braided rugs to enhance the country appeal. Place area rugs under or beside the bed for added comfort, and use them to define an intimate seating area.

✧✦✧

RIGHT, TOP: Plush carpeting not only contributes color and luxurious texture but helps soundproof the bedroom. This beautiful Victorian sanctuary boasts a striking bed and dresser accessorized with favorite items and period-perfect lamps. Lace curtains, needlepoint throw rugs, flowers, family photos, and a lovely quilt atop the bed are the details that make the difference.

RIGHT, BOTTOM: This rustic attic retreat has romantic and relaxed country Victorian appeal. Whitewashed plank walls and blond wooden flooring provide a serene backdrop for an artistic blend of furnishings that includes upholstered period chairs, a round white table, and a marble-topped table brightened with a coat of blue paint. Black and white geometric area rugs anchor the bedroom with bold pattern while soft white bedding, framed vintage embroidered linens, and a ruffled footstool add soft touches.

Lighting

Lighting in the traditional bedroom usually takes the form of general and task lighting. A lovely ceiling fixture, perhaps combined with a quality ceiling fan, is perfect in warmer climates. Where a ceiling fan is not required for comfort, a glass fixture in a pendant or teardrop shape will contribute subtle ambience. Other ceiling fixtures are available in a variety of styles with different decorative effects. Choose the one that best suits your needs and brings elegance as well as light to your traditional-style bedroom. If your bedroom is quite large, consider a beautiful chandelier for formal and stately appeal.

Task lighting in the bedroom usually consists of one or more lamps for reading, lighting located near a dresser or dressing table, and closet lighting. A bedside table outfitted with a lamp is a must for relaxing at night with a good book before actually turning in. Make sure the lamp is tall enough to provide ample light for reading, and select a light that serves as a "furnishing" in that it complements the bedroom's decor. Lovely wall sconces flanking a headboard can also be used for task lighting, provided they cast light downward or are adjustable. Wall lamps with adjustable swing arms can serve the same purpose.

Grooming and applying makeup require a source of bright but diffused light at the dressing table or dresser. Lighting in the form of either a tabletop lamp or sconces with opaque shades is ideal. The closet requires sufficient lighting from a ceiling or wall fixture, so that you don't have to fumble in the shadows to find that favorite outfit and the pair of shoes that matches it.

Personal style, the traditional decor of your bedroom, and your particular lighting needs will ultimately determine your selections. Keep in mind that decorative details make all the difference in a room with timeless appeal. Select your lighting fixtures carefully, with your color scheme and decorating theme in mind. Fixtures can be simple and elegant, romantic, or polished and ornate.

ABOVE: The bed naturally becomes the focal point in any bedroom, so it's good to have a handsome example to ground the decor. This lovely Renaissance Revival–style bed is placed against dramatic red walls and dressed with soft red and blue bedding. An octagonal black bedside table with gilt ornamentation holds a striking and unique spherical lamp with a classic black shade. The framed architectural prints over the bed and the miniature frieze are in keeping with the neoclassical theme of the room.

OPPOSITE: White on white works wonders in this enchanting bedroom. Crisp white walls and puffy bedding (sans headboard) create an almost minimalist decor, but a Victorian lady's chair with a rich, striped fabric adds a touch of traditional style. Tall iron candelabra flank the bedstead for bedtime stories, and a vibrant still life provides a necessary spot of color.

Window Treatments

The windows in a traditional-style bedroom can be graciously dressed for maximum beauty and privacy or provided with a light covering that is more open and airy. Controlling light is a primary concern in regard to window treatments in the bedroom, and the fabric and color used at the windows should relate in some fashion to the bed dressing.

For a more formal, elegant bedroom, draperies made of chintz, brocade, or taffeta can be used in tandem with swags or valances to impart a luxurious effect. To provide maximum comfort, determine whether or not draperies should be lined to control sunlight streaming through and to protect costly fabrics. Consider matching the drapery fabric with bed curtains, a padded fabric headboard, a bedspread, or upholstery fabric on chairs or pillows.

In the bedroom where strong natural lighting is of little concern, windows can be dressed with beautiful curtains looped back and held in place with a classic rosette. Use a sheer fabric window shade underneath or an elegant lace panel to heighten the decorative appeal.

Draw draperies can command attention in a traditional bedroom when they are custom-crafted from a sumptuous fabric and bedecked with tassels or fringe. Tie them back with tasseled cords or braiding and use a fabric roller shade underneath for maximum privacy.

For less formal bedrooms, especially a guest room or a child's bedroom, window treatments can be scaled down while still providing definite style. Rather than using floor-length draperies, draw curtains pulled to the side with fabric tiebacks or café curtains on brass rings make a nice alternative. Lace panels accessorized with a chintz valance add a soft touch to a girl's room or a bedroom with nineteenth-century ambience.

Shades are a convenient window treatment in any number of traditional decorating schemes. Fabric Roman shades are a no-fuss means of providing style that's both decorative and functional. A dressy balloon shade, on the other hand, has a definite Victorian air and is perfect in a feminine bedroom. Bamboo shades combined with a striking valance work well in the traditional bedroom that takes its cue from the Orient, and all-purpose vinyl blinds or mini blinds used with a valance or swag are adaptable to any number of casual traditional bedrooms. Painted wooden shutters with fabric trim, such as a valance or swag, are popular in a traditional setting.

❧❧❧

OPPOSITE: Window treatments can impart strong style in the traditional bedroom—from the hopelessly romantic to a more tailored or casual look. The windows in this gracious bedroom are dressed with custom-made draperies that emphasize the architectural lines. A beautiful chintz swag fashioned with a rosette gives each window a soft, finishing touch that bespeaks period style.

ABOVE: A lovely floral pattern graces the wallpaper, bed curtains, and window treatment, creating an elegant yet romantic look in this bedroom. Simple white bed linens and neutral carpeting keep the room from feeling cluttered. Classic furniture designs and the decorative effect achieved by a skirted bedside table make this inviting sanctuary complete.

ABOVE: Soft, nature-inspired colors and yards of fabric have been used to design a bedroom with elegant Asian undertones. A stunning antique wardrobe provides plenty of space to store clothes and extra bedding, while a kilim softens the dark hardwood floor. Tailored valances—on the canopy bed and at the windows—serve as fitting accessories for lovely draperies that puddle at the floor. Overstuffed easy chairs provide a welcome spot to relax.

RIGHT: A delicately painted dressing table and matching chair make a fitting addition to an elegant bedroom. Placed in the corner, this lovely set allows the owner to take advantage of the view outside either window. In keeping with the spirit of a formal traditional style, the windows have been lavished with lace panels and the draperies accessorized with tasseled fringe and tiebacks.

Furnishings

When it comes to discussing furniture for the traditional bedroom, naturally the first thing to come to mind is the bed. A handsome four-poster bed is the epitome of formal period style. In a luxurious bedroom, a four-poster can be dressed with an arrangement of bed curtains that are purely for show. Consisting of a fabric canopy, valance, and curtains that puddle at the floor (which can surround the bed or be tied back at all four corners), this treatment works especially well with luxurious printed fabrics. The valance used in fashioning bed curtains will set the decorative tone, whether it is tailored, pleated, or bedecked with tassels and fringe. Keep this in mind when selecting window dressings and coordinate the two for an elegant look.

Variations on the bed curtain for a four-poster bed include a scaled-down treatment consisting of a canopy, valance, and floor-length curtains tied back at the head of the bed only. This is every bit as lovely as a full curtain treatment, but it provides for more openness and requires a great deal less fabric.

A similar effect can also be achieved without the benefit of a four-poster bed. For example, a bed with a striking fabric headboard can be decorated with a half-circle coronet or crown dressing suspended from the wall behind the bed. From this crown or coronet, elegant folds of fabric cascade down behind the headboard and along the sides of the head of the bed. These side curtains can then be arranged in place with beautiful rosettes, bows, or tiebacks. A half-canopy treatment would be similar, but rectangular rather than rounded.

A French-inspired sleigh bed is ideal for a neoclassical bedroom, and it can also be dressed with a bed curtain for decorative flair. When dealing with a single bed, place it lengthwise against a wall, and mount a decorative pole near the ceiling from which you can hang a beautiful length of fabric that will drape toward both the headboard and footboard. Wall-mounted rosettes at either end will allow the fabric to fan out and billow to the floor.

Of course, stately four-posters or classic sleigh beds look perfectly wonderful without bed curtains and can still impart a formal air. Look for an elegant bedspread and patterned dust ruffle or bed skirt (if called for) to serve as highly decorative details.

Naturally, there are other beds in period or classic styles that are ideally suited to a traditional decor. For Victorian ambience, look for an antique or reproduction bed with an ornately carved headboard and footboard. An elegant brass or iron bed will also speak of the gilded age. In contrast, simplicity can be found in a handsome oak or cherry bed crafted in the Arts and Crafts style, or in a pencil-post bed reminiscent of Shaker designs. Traditional country style allows for the use of low four-poster beds and cannonball beds that hint at a more casual—even rustic—decor.

Dressers and chests of drawers are needed in the bedroom to provide adequate storage for those items that shouldn't hang in a closet. A Queen Anne high chest or Chippendale chest-on-chest can be used along with a smaller bombé or serpentine-front chest for a truly period look. Classic styling calls to mind Federal or Empire case pieces that will enhance a neoclassical decor. Elegant lacquered chests will give your sanctuary an exotic flavor. For a formal Victorian look, consider a marble-topped dresser. Finally, traditional bedrooms that boast country roots often make use of an assortment of honey pine case pieces or painted cottage-style furniture.

Bedside tables need not necessarily match the bed. Queen Anne tea tables might be ideal, or perhaps you prefer simple round tables covered with decorative fabric puddling at the floor. Add a protective glass top, and place books and other creature comforts close at hand. Nightstands come in many different styles that are suitable for a traditional decor

Since bedrooms are no longer used solely for sleep, you may want to include a handsome desk for personal papers, a cabinet or armoire for the television set, and comfy chairs for reading and relaxing. An upholstered easy chair with a matching ottoman is the ideal place for escape. A Grecian daybed or wicker chaise longue dressed with throw pillows will provide the ultimate spot for indulgent moments of peace and quiet—or a catnap. Above all, allow your own personal style to be the guiding force in outfitting your traditional-style bedroom.

OPPOSITE: A handsome four-poster bed dressed with a white bed skirt and woven coverlet is the star of this Colonial-style bedroom. Gray-blue paint defines the window moldings in typical period style, while casual white curtains are dressed up with ribbon trim and tiebacks. The framed sampler on the wall and the collection of antique quilts speak of the owner's appreciation of fine needlework.

LEFT: In this traditional bedroom, the furnishings—a beautiful sleigh bed, handsome armoire, and French Provençal chair—convey old-world style. A red and white toile de Jouy fabric, a hallmark of French Provençal style, has been used for the draperies, bedding, and upholstery. Tassels, topiaries, and an urn-shaped lamp give this stunning bedroom a finished look.

ABOVE: A contemporary interpretation of a traditional design can be quite striking, such as this four-poster bed crafted from sleek black metal. The Federal-style armchair and handsome chest of drawers recall the past in a more common manner. Windows are formally dressed with elegant swags and jabots atop floor-length draperies to give the room an elegant air.

Accessories

Details, details, details: they have proven time and again to be the determining factor in creating a stunning room. Even very small details can have a big impact, especially in the bedroom. For example, consider your bed and how it will be dressed. Rich fabrics have long been associated with a formal and elegant decor, so if your traditional setting aspires to create this particular mood, cover your bed with a sumptuous bedspread, pillows, decorative throw pillows, and a bed skirt.

Romance in the classic bedroom can be subtly conveyed via crisp white linens and yards of lace. Flowery chintz used in combination with lace has a definite Victorian flavor. Hand-embroidered linens are the perfect match for a Mission-style oak bed. Crewelwork bedspreads recall period style, as do toile de Jouy fabrics used for bedspreads or curtains. Either fabric can be appropriate for a formal or more relaxed setting.

For casual country ambience, think quilts. You can accessorize an antique or a quality replica with a dust ruffle and pillows for old-fashioned charm. Striped ticking is another low-key yet striking means of adding color and pattern to a country bed.

What next? Take a look around the bedroom. Surely you have the perfect crystal, silver, or crockery vase for a fresh bouquet of flowers. By all means, bring the outdoors inside and surround yourself with your favorite flowers and fragrances. And you needn't stop there. Botanical prints are also lovely in the bedroom.

Since the traditional-style bedroom is a safe haven—a truly personal space to call your own—surround yourself with cherished mementos, precious family photographs, and favorite keepsakes. A collection of beautiful perfume bottles, for example, is perfect for a tablescape or an arrangement on the dressing table. Be creative. After all, you have only to please yourself.

OPPOSITE: When it comes to bedroom furniture, nothing says traditional style like a beautiful canopy bed. This wonderful example has a delicately carved and curved frame covered with a crocheted canopy. The lovely patchwork spread has a timeless appeal, as do the hardwood floor and simple drapery treatment.

RIGHT: Deep red walls and a white molded cornice define this gracious bedroom. The beautiful bed, accessorized with a half-canopy, displays folds of lace and a red and white scalloped valance with tieback curtains. Coordinated bedding completes the traditional setting. A round, skirted table serves as a bedside stand, and an eye-catching vignette is designed from family photos, flowers, and a silver dresser set.

ABOVE: Soft color and subtle textures define this lovely traditional bedroom. White beadboard paneling and pale blue walls are restful and relaxing, while the ornate metal headboard, wicker baskets, and the handsome wooden dresser create a pleasing contrast. Elegant white bedding provides understated beauty.

LEFT: Sweet dreams and solid comfort are to be found in this traditional bedroom. The sumptuous bed sports a striped, fabric-covered headboard and footboard and is piled high with pillows and a white comforter. The bedside table keeps books, flowers, and a lovely silver lamp close at hand. A delicate tapestry-inspired wallpaper in light, neutral hues adds elegance and Victorian-era style.

OPPOSITE: A soothing neutral palette in this charming bedroom is given a touch of country color and pattern with a blue and white checkered bedspread. A rustic built-in wardrobe and a classical fireplace add architectural interest, while the oval gilt-framed mirror offers a dressy, traditional touch. The bouquet of flowers and the porcelain jars atop the mantel continue the blue and white theme.

Chapter Seven
THE BATHROOM

The modern-day bathroom, in many homes, has come full circle, and often resembles the luxurious baths that made their debut in Victorian homes of the nineteenth century. But luxury has not always been the case, and the technological and industrial advances that made the bathroom possible were preceded by decades of makeshift apparatuses and less-than-ideal bathing conditions.

Throughout history, especially in ancient times, bathing was equated with purity and physical strength. It was also widely recognized for its healing properties, and bathing itself was a ritualistic indulgence performed on a regular basis.

The significance of bathing during the early industrial period was overshadowed by more immediate concerns, such as survival, food, and shelter, but as time passed, personal hygiene took on increased importance. By the late eighteenth century, the larger homes of the wealthy had a private dressing room off the chamber or bedroom, where bathing and the "daily toilette" could be performed. This dressing room was frequently outfitted as a small sitting room might be, complete with a comfortable chair, a chest of drawers, a dressing table, and a washstand. A fireplace was imperative in the dressing room for comfort, and a portable tub could be placed here for a full bath. In some homes, however, the tub was located in a separate "bathroom" designed specifically for bathing. Such an arrangement was not the norm; most of the population made do with more primitive measures, and the daily toilette, which included a lukewarm sponge bath, was conducted rather hastily in the bedroom in the morning or at night.

Attention to personal hygiene came to be equated with gentility and good moral standing by the early 1800s, and instructional behavioral guides as well as myriad etiquette manuals stressed the importance of cleanliness. As early as the 1860s, some rather progressive city homes had bathrooms with permanent tubs and hot- and cold-water taps. A "water closet," on the

OPPOSITE: Significant decorative touches give this traditional bath charming character. A claw-foot tub and pedestal sink impart Victorian style, but a stunning overmantel mirror lends this bath a signature touch. A stained-glass window propped on the ledge and a vintage scale add a sense of whimsy.

ABOVE: Attention to detail has created a traditional look in this bath. Walls are papered with a serene botanical pattern, and a coordinating fabric has been used for the curtains at the wide window. The vintage tub has been given a fresh coat of paint in a traditional color and fitted with elegant brass hardware.

other hand, was virtually unheard of indoors for most homes, and the outhouse still served as the toilet. Those with delicate constitutions who were hesitant to venture outdoors, especially at night, relied upon china chamber pots and slop buckets, which were standard equipment in the Victorian boudoir. Victorian sensibilities dictated that these necessary items be hidden away under beds or placed in special case pieces called commodes, where a small cupboard kept them handy but removed from sight. On top of the commode was the pitcher and basin used for sponge bathing. Sometimes a washstand with a towel rack was used instead.

By the late 1800s, urban areas had access to plumbing lines, and the bathroom as we know it was born. Victorians often devoted a bedroom-size space to the bath, and the room was not only quite large but luxurious in its appointments. Elegant and embellished sinks, tubs, and toilets were often encased in fine mahogany and accessorized with brass trim and hardware. A fine Oriental rug was often laid upon the floor, and with the fireplace and a comfortable chair close at hand, the bathroom was as lovely and elegant as any other room in the house. The bathroom, in fact, was a status symbol of sorts, one that the Victorians were proud to show off to their friends.

The focus on sanitary measures and the call to simplify many areas of daily life resulted in smaller bathrooms by the turn of the century. These bathrooms, however, were not without decorative charm. Gleaming pedestal sinks, claw-foot tubs, and glossy white wall tiles were used in combination with etched or art glass windows and easy-care surfaces. For the most part, the bath had become practical and functional, but its simplicity also resulted in beauty.

Decorating today's bathroom in a traditional style is similar to doing up the kitchen: we call upon the essence of the style—found in materials, colors, decorative

effects, and popular motifs—to express timeless beauty. And we have the added advantage of seeing the bath as a private retreat, where pampering need know no bounds.

Regardless of whether your bathroom is small or decadently large, it can be designed, remodeled, or simply spruced up for maximum practicality, comfort, and decorative appeal. If you have space for a large whirlpool tub, an enclosed shower, and double sinks at the vanity, wonderful! If not, even the most basic bathroom can function as a welcoming, relaxing retreat.

Two views of this Victorian-inspired bath showcase its tremendous appeal.
OPPOSITE: His-and-hers pedestal sinks make the bath as convenient as it is lovely.
A handsome wood-framed mirror creates a striking focal point that conveys timeless design, and monogrammed towels lend an elegant, personal touch.
ABOVE: A white beadboard wainscot and tub enclosure, along with the tiled backsplash, form the all-important crisp, clean-looking background. Lace curtains and a soft floral rug add beauty and texture, and details, such as the upholstered stool and the antique plant stand, fill the room with period style.

Wall Treatments

Start by considering the shell of your bathroom. A notable ceiling cornice will add architectural flair. From there, give thought to your walls. The bathroom has special needs given the moisture and humidity that are ever-present, so make sure your paint or wallpaper is suitable. If you opt for a wooden wainscot (perhaps beadboard paneling), it can be painted or treated with a durable finish. Tile and marble are a natural choice for the bathroom, as they are easy to clean and maintain.

Color and pattern have strong decorative impact in the traditional-inspired bath. Muted, medium to dark hues will enhance the relaxing qualities of the bath, while bright colors and pastels create an open, airy look and make a small space appear larger. White is ideal for a traditional bath and can be teamed up with an accent color, or made all the more lovely with gleaming trim and hardware. As always, neutrals adapt well to a traditional decor.

The versatility of paint should not be overlooked when it comes to the bathroom. You can decorate walls with your favorite color, or you can go one

step beyond and create a faux finish by painting walls for a softly aged look, embellishing them with a stencil design, or imitating stone or even marble. Paint can also be used in combination with wallpaper, tile, or wainscoting for a division of wall space. Or you can simply accent painted walls with a decorative wallpaper border.

Never underestimate the decorative powers of wallpaper in a small space. Even the most diminutive bathroom can command attention when walls take on a pleasing pattern. For a traditional period look, think stripes or floral motifs. Neoclassical design can be conveyed by choosing a wallpaper with a repeating pattern of ancient themes or patriotic images. Florals, paisley, and mini prints are ideal in a Victorian or countrified bath. Stylized motifs from nature will recall the Art Nouveau or Arts and Crafts movements, and wallpaper with an Oriental design will contribute an exotic touch in a traditional bath.

If cost is not an important factor in planning or redecorating the bath, beautifully colored tiles can be used on walls. White tiles are the obvious choice to re-create late-nineteenth-century ambience, but even this period setting can be elevated to an art form by incorporating a few hand-painted or patterned tiles for a rich effect. Tile trim in an accent color can also be used to define spaces.

❦

OPPOSITE: Casual country touches make this Depression-era bathroom inviting. Light green tiles and pink paint adorn the walls, while a nubby rag rug softens the tile floor. A vintage tub and pedestal sink are reminiscent of days gone by, as is the oak sideboard that has cleverly been put to use as a storage cupboard. The matching green wicker chair, framed prints, and dried flowers are cheerful, homey additions.
RIGHT: The essence of traditional style is clearly conveyed in this attractive bath, where tile reigns supreme. Apricot tile flooring and an apricot and white checkered wainscot are joined by a matching tile tub surround. Brass faucets and fixtures, including a towel bar, add an elegant touch. A reproduction light fixture on the mirror and a handsome vintage-style sink recall the past.

Floor Treatments

Bathroom floors should be practical, but they can also be striking and beautiful. Marble tiles are expensive but long-lasting, and will instantly imbue the bathroom with traditional appeal. The same effect can be achieved by installing ceramic tile with the look of marble. There are so many color and pattern choices when it comes to tile that it's well worth spending some time at a store that specializes in these products. Tiles are available in several sizes, and depending upon the square footage of your floor, you can opt for one-inch (2.5cm) mosaic tiles mounted on a mesh backing or go with something larger, such as twelve-by-twelve-inch (30.5 by 30.5cm) tiles. Square mosaic tiles in a black and white (or blue and white or green and white) pattern are a lovely addition to the traditional bath. If your decorating scheme is rooted in the late nineteenth century, mosaic tiles in a hexagon pattern will instantly impart Victorian spirit. If, on the other hand, larger tiles are preferred, design an elegant border or central floral or geometric motif. The opportunities to design a "floorscape" are endless and should not be overlooked. One word of caution: shop for unglazed tiles or tiles with a matte finish, as these are less prone to becoming slippery when wet. For safety, add a nonskid rug in front of the shower or bathtub.

Resilient flooring is also quite practical in the traditional bathroom, and as with tile, there are so many colors and patterns available today that you should have no problem finding something to complement your decorating scheme. Available as square tiles or in sheets, resilient flooring is cost-efficient and requires only minimal upkeep. Choose a solid vinyl flooring for longevity, and check manufacturer recommendations for proper cleaning.

A wood floor can be adapted to the traditional bath, provided the floor is properly sealed and wet spots are mopped up right away. A hardwood floor can contribute a rich, formal look in a traditional bath if accessorized with a handsome area rug. In contrast, country spirit will reign supreme if plank flooring is painted, stenciled, or simply covered with a thick rag rug for softness underfoot.

ABOVE: This charming Victorian bath is a favorite retreat for indulging the spirit and the senses. Resilient flooring with a tile pattern and walls with beadboard wainscoting and floral wallpaper make a pleasing background for an old-fashioned claw-foot tub. A small antique washstand provides an attractive spot for toiletries. Such subtle details as ruffled window curtains, a collection of antique toiletry bottles, and fresh tulips are in keeping with the period theme.

ABOVE: A warm bath awaits, and the surroundings couldn't be more inviting. This sizable bathroom is a study in neutral hues, from the pale peach walls to the subtle grays and browns of the tile floor. The pedestal sink has a custom-built vanity with plenty of drawers, and the bath is outfitted with gleaming brass hardware. Flowers, a framed print, and a cushioned metal stool contribute subtle beauty.

Lighting

To achieve solid comfort in the traditional bathroom, make adequate lighting a top priority. General and task lighting are called for, and both can be introduced via out-of-the-way recessed fixtures. Consider having them installed not only in the center of the room but near the vanity, sink, or grooming area as well.

General lighting in the traditional bathroom can also take a dramatic role in creating an appealing decor. For a spacious, elegant bathroom, you can add the ultimate lighting fixture—a chandelier—to boldly reveal an elaborate or patrician decorating scheme. More often than not, however, a simpler ceiling fixture, such as a beautiful glass example with brass trim or a striking painted shade, will suffice. A fixture that includes a ceiling fan can help reduce humidity.

To make sure you have sufficient light at the sink or vanity for grooming or other needs, add a wall-mounted light above the mirror. Better yet, situate a light on either side of the mirror to avoid glare. Wall sconces are ideal for this type of setup and can take many different decorative forms. Shell-shaped sconces are perfect for imparting classic style, as are miniature candlestick lamps with attractive fabric shades. For something with Victorian flair, frosted or etched glass globes fill the bill. Linear copper or other metal fixtures with slag glass would be a wonderful addition to an Arts and Crafts–inspired bath. Shop carefully at the lighting fixture stores and sources for wonderful ideas and inspiring ways to add style to the bath.

ABOVE: This small but lovely bathroom receives plenty of natural light during the day. At night, a porcelain wall sconce provides light where it's needed most—by the mirror. An old-fashioned claw-foot tub and a handsome antique sink with brass hardware make this bath into a peaceful retreat. Simple decorative elements, such as the sea shells lined up on the window sill, the glass full of just-picked flowers on the sink, and the wicker hamper add a personal touch.

Window Treatments

Bathroom windows offer a world of possibilities for decorative details in a traditional bath. At its most basic, a bathroom with a splendid view and total privacy can be left bare to allow the beauty of the outdoors to come in.

This is especially striking when the bathroom plays host to a Palladian window, a round window, an oval window, or some other equally pleasing architectural design. The Victorians, of course, took this feature one step further and created art glass windows that were beautiful, functional, and quite striking in the bath. These decorative elements can be re-created today with elegant nineteenth-century style.

In the majority of homes, however, a compromise must be reached between allowing natural light into the bath and providing for solitary comfort. Still, options in regard to bathroom window dressings are more numerous than you might think. Keep in mind that you'll want something easy to maintain and strong enough to withstand the special conditions in the bath. Heavy fabrics at the window often prove to be a poor choice because they retain moisture. Rather, it is advantageous to think "light and airy." Cotton fabrics, sheers, or lace panels are ideal. You can accessorize them with a valance or swag, or allow the elegance of simplicity to stand alone. You can also make a simple curtain treatment more noticeable by using a decorative rod and finials.

Louvered shutters, wooden blinds, and vinyl blinds are practical alternatives to curtains in the traditional bath. For something a bit different and perhaps dressy, wooden shutters can be enhanced with printed fabric inserts.

Fabric shades or Roman shades are an excellent choice in the traditional bath, where they convey classic style and prove ideal for controlling light. They can be decidedly elegant, tailored, or plain; it's all a matter of your taste and the level of decoration you wish to achieve. For the Victoriana enthusiast, puffy balloon shades will add to the period style.

Similar in design, but serving a different purpose, is the fabric used for a shower curtain, to enclose a tub, or to act as skirting around a sink. Fabrics can be coordinated to create a unifying effect in the bath, so consider matching any of the above to a window dressing. In the case of a shower curtain, be sure to use a waterproof liner.

LEFT: Simplicity can be beautiful, especially in a bathroom that features vintage fixtures and honey-colored wood flooring. To add to this charming effect, airy, sheer curtains have been selected to dress the window and thick, soft toweling is conveniently placed on a nearby metal rack.

ABOVE: With a dramatic and private view like this, there's no need for a window treatment. Streamlined fixtures with elegant, arched hardware and simple white tiles create a modern bath with classic charm.

Fixtures

When it comes to outfitting the bathroom, think of fixtures as you would furnishings. Function and practicality are important considerations, but so, too, is beauty. Today there are more beautiful choices than ever. The size of your bathroom will have the most impact on the fixtures you choose, but consider them with an eye toward convenience, comfort, and decorative appeal as well.

Bathtubs can be quite basic or large and luxurious with whirlpool action. While we tend to think of white for the bathroom, tubs and other fixtures are available today in a rainbow of colors. Also, ask yourself if the tub will be encased in wood, a tile surround, or marble. Cost is an important factor, along with your decorating scheme.

Perhaps you have visions of a lovely claw-foot tub. This is a must in the Victorian-period bath, and many such tubs are available in modern-day reproductions. Anyone with their heart set on a vintage claw-foot tub should check it carefully to determine the condition and level of restoration or repair that might be called for. Be aware, too, that vintage tubs are very heavy and, depending on the condition of your floors, may not be suitable for second-story bathrooms.

Toilets are also sold in a wide range of colors and styles. Do you prefer a streamlined model or the good old standard? Fortunately, current models are designed for optimum efficiency with water-saving features. Again, let your personal style be your guide.

Of all the fixtures called for in the bath, the sink probably allows the most creative leeway. Just imagine incorporating a beautiful china sink with a hand-painted floral or foliage motif into your traditional bath. A shell-shaped sink is also a lovely and subtle way of adding a popular traditional motif to a period-inspired setting. Then, too, you can always have a sink placed in a striking piece of furniture. A notable sideboard, a marble-topped dresser, or even a pine commode can become a custom-crafted vanity. The advantage here, of course, is that you have both good looks and abundant storage space.

For those who prefer a pedestal design or need to consider one due to space constraints, this type of sink can also point to period style. A pedestal sink with a column base is certainly a classical form. Other bases imitate pillars or slender stands. Let your personal taste guide your decision. For those who aspire to re-create a crisp, white turn-of-the-century bath,

reproduction fixtures are available, or you can scout the architectural salvage emporiums for the real thing.

Bathroom fixtures need hardware, and this is no small detail when creating traditional ambience. To imbue the bath with richness and luxury, sparkling brass faucets will do the trick. For a more casual air, glass knobs or porcelain and brass knobs are a bit more relaxed. Variety is the key word in regard to hardware for the bath, so be sure to visit a specialty store to better appreciate the selection available today.

BELOW: Classic styling is obvious in this stunning bath. Stone tiles in a variety of warm earth tones surround the inviting tub with elegance. Shiny brass hardware is in keeping with this well-appointed setting and adds just the right touch of formality.

Accessories

Bathroom accessories can go a long way toward conveying decorative style. If room allows, include a classic chair for seating or for storage. A small side chair with a neoclassical lyre back and a lovely upholstered seat will do nicely, and don't worry if no one actually uses it for sitting: it can be just as beautiful when used to hold a stack of towels. A small table or chest of drawers in a period style can always be used in the bath to hide linens, and the top can hold assorted grooming items. A bamboo whatnot shelf will keep bathroom necessities close at hand and add a dose of Oriental design. A large mirror is a must in the bath, and a gilded example can be beautiful. Be creative; a traditional bathroom derives style from decorative period elements used in imaginative ways.

For the bathroom with a more relaxed air and the flavor of traditional country style, a painted chest of drawers or a wall-hung cupboard may be the perfect addition to your decor. Wicker, whether in the form of a table, chair, or chest, can contribute Victorian flair. And for the Arts and Crafts admirer, oak accessories with clean lines make the perfect accoutrements, as they are a hallmark of that particular style.

Who says bric-a-brac has no place in the traditional bath? As with the other rooms in the home, you want to avoid clutter, but artfully arranged collections are definitely a plus. Think of grouping framed prints, paintings, or photographs on a bathroom wall. A shelf or vanity top can be transformed into an elegant vignette with a collection of antique perfume bottles or a silver dresser set. Since today we consider the bathroom a space for relaxing and pampering ourselves, by all means, surround yourself with the objects you love.

Bathroom linens are necessities, but they, too, can have strong decorative impact. When it comes to towels, purchase quality stock that is thick, soft, and durable. Place attractive hooks on the door or wall for extra space to hang towels.

Fresh flowers are a nice touch in the traditional bath, but green plants will thrive in this moisture-rich setting. Ferns especially like the humidity and warmth found in the bathroom. A window ledge or tabletop will do nicely for a display spot.

Finally, add your favorite soaps, lotions, and other grooming items so that they'll always be close at hand. Light a scented candle, draw a warm bath, relax, and enjoy.

ABOVE: Favorite photos and framed prints cover the walls of this handsome English-style bath. Dark wooden furnishings, such as the corner cabinet housing the sink and the spool-turned shelf for linens, have a formal appeal that's complemented by the plush rug and select toiletries and accessories.

OPPOSITE: The bathroom often functions as a personal haven for relaxation and much-needed pampering. Here, elements of classic design—from the tiled walls to the Roman shade at the window—create a sumptuous bath enhanced with pleasing accessories. With the addition of a scented candle, a metal lyre-back chair, flowers, and a snack of fresh fruit, this bath becomes a place to indulge in stolen moments.

Chapter Eight

Chapter Eight

OUTDOOR SPACES

Serving as an extension of the home, outdoor spaces have long been enjoyed as places for rest, relaxation, family gatherings and activities, and the opportunity to savor the delights of warm weather and the fresh splendor of nature.

As far back as ancient Babylon and Rome, people were cultivating gardens filled with plants that were useful for cooking and healing. By the Renaissance, ornamental plants that were beautiful rather than useful began to appear in the stylised, symmetrical gardens of the day. Before common architectural styles allowed for piazzas or porches, people would retire to the garden or under the shade of a tree for afternoon tea, a visit with guests, or perhaps a light meal. Only the well-to-do could afford to devote time to formal flower gardening during the 1700s, but even members of the growing middle class had favorite spots in the yard or on the front stoop to revel in the cool breezes or soft sunshine. And not surpsrisingly, furniture advertised for the outdoors was being sold by urban cabinetmakers during the early eighteenth century. For the most part these "garden" furnishings were Windsor chairs and small, lightweight tables that could easily be moved indoors.

By the early 1800s, many homes in warm, southern areas were being constructed with wide piazzas, large covered porches that were furnished and outfitted for maximum comfort and pleasure during the long, hot summer months. Floorcloths occasionally dressed the wood floor; venetian blinds or billowing fabrics acted as curtains to filter the sun's rays; and assorted tables, benches, and chairs were scattered about for family and friends.

A covered piazza both cooled the interior of the home and provided a sheltered outdoor space, and early-nineteenth-century house designs continued to incorporate such a feature. Greek Revival–style homes often included a columned portico or porch, and Victorian architectural styles from the Gothic Revival to Queen Anne took the front porch to new heights of decorative embellishment.

During the Victorian period, outdoor living became commonplace, and the middle class furnished their porches and informal cottage-style gardens with appointments as lovely as those found inside the home. This was, after all, the age of decorative excess. The Windsor furnishings used outdoors

OPPOSITE: A covered section of this stone patio becomes the perfect outdoor space for relaxed meals. Painted wicker chairs with plump yellow and white striped cushions are gathered about a rustic table that's set for lunch. A festive flowered tablecloth helps create a summery table setting, and even the ivy-patterned dishes continue the garden theme.
ABOVE: A gazebo is a wonderful addition to any garden sanctuary. When furnished with a casual wicker table and chairs, it can be used for alfresco meals with the family, or it can be outfitted with a comfortable weatherproof couch for curling up with a good book or dozing in the sun.

during the eighteenth century gave way to ornate cast-iron chairs and settees that were popular in the garden during the mid-1800s. More rustic wooden benches and chairs were also used. The quintessential porch furnishing material—wicker—made its debut during the second half of the nineteenth century, and later, wirework furnishings were produced. Wicker, however, was not only comfortable and adaptable to a variety of forms, it was also weather-resistant.

During the late nineteenth century and into the twentieth century, wicker could be found on the porch, in the sunroom or conservatory, and even in the parlor. Wicker furnishings were turned out in styles ranging from ornate (Victorian) to streamlined (Arts and Crafts) and although its popularity waned for several decades, wicker is once again in vogue, just as it was a century ago.

Along with the porch, other outdoor spaces captured the imaginations of our ancestors, including the secluded garden sanctuary complete with a trellised seating area and, later, the gazebo. The porch, however, reigned supreme through the early 1900s, when even bungalow architecture provided a sheltered porch space with a low-pitched roof design. Several decades later the move to the suburbs was under way, and popular home styles traded the front porch for the seclusion of the backyard patio or deck.

Today, we seem to have come full circle: homes are once again being built or remodeled with a front porch for easy outdoor living. Many homes also maintain a backyard space for enjoyment, whether it be a garden, patio, or deck. Even those homes or apartments that don't have the benefit of a porch or patio may include an airy sunroom or conservatory. With this in mind, careful attention to detail will render a glorious outdoor space that can be used as an enjoyable and relaxing extension of the home.

ABOVE: A rustic stone patio becomes a wonderful outdoor living space when outfitted with classic Adirondack chairs and a cheery red Windsor settee. Clay pots filled with geraniums and baskets full of flowers gathered from the nearby garden are natural forms of decoration. A blue checkered cloth adorns a tiny table used for refreshments.
OPPOSITE: This exquisite tiled patio is enhanced with potted plants and cheery bougainvillea blossoms, which spill over the beams of the latticed roof. Architectural details, seen in the handsome square column and decorative iron gate, recall traditional, old-world style. A weathered wicker chair and ornate Islamic stand encourage sitting a spell with a good book.

Ceilings and Floors

The front porch is typically made of wood, but modern materials also allow for columns and trim created of weather- and insect-resistant compounds. These are available through dealers who specialize in architectural products. Color is naturally a key factor in decorating the porch so that it enhances the look of your home and creates a welcoming outdoor spot. The porch ceiling is often white, but you might consider painting it a pale blue to imitate the sky, as was done in centuries past. Other color options include nature-inspired hues for the porch floor, such as sand, gray, or green. Make sure the paints you use are weather-resistant and appropriate to the porch. Once painted, accessorize the floor with an easy-care sisal matting to define an intimate grouping of chairs. For a countrified look, consider casual rag rugs. A more formal air can be achieved by adding a small geometric or Oriental rug, provided it is protected from the elements.

Brick or flagstone patios display their own beauty and charm, but for the backyard deck made of pressure-treated lumber, you'll want to apply a water-resistant sealer or paint to prolong the life of the structure. Add a scatter rug or two for comfort and style.

RIGHT: This classic front porch is defined by handsome and stately Doric columns. Furnished with airy wicker pieces, the porch invites relaxation in the beauty of the great outdoors. The white wicker chairs and sofa are dressed with blue cushions for added comfort, and a low plank table serves up snacks and cool beverages.
OPPOSITE: A columned balcony becomes a cozy outdoor retreat when comfortable, overstuffed furnishings beckon. Rattan chairs and matching ottomans are cleverly placed to create a pair of chaise longues, perfect for sitting and enjoying the landscaped garden.

ABOVE: This home has no front porch, but the owners have created a miniature patio that serves the same function. The trim on the house gives the impression of a trellis when potted rose trees are placed in front of it. White Adirondack chairs flank the doorway, creating a perfect spot to relax in the sun. Simplicity can be lovely when classics are called into play.

Lighting and Shade

To provide maximum comfort on a porch with a sunny exposure, shades or blinds that can be rolled up and out of sight when not in use are a necessity. Bamboo matchstick blinds or wooden blinds are ideal, but there are other options available today. You can use white or striped fabric shades for a dressy touch, or you may prefer the look of latticework, which also serves as a climbing trellis for flowering vines.

The backyard deck or patio can be handsomely outfitted with a fabric awning (again, stripes are perfect for the traditional home), and a tailored or scalloped valance can be added to heighten the decorative effect.

Soft lighting for the porch can be achieved with a period ceiling or hanging fixture or, on the porch or patio, sconces that flank the front or back door. Choose the fixtures to correspond with the architectural styling of your home, and use bug-deterring lightbulbs during warm weather months. For relaxing evenings spent outdoors, candlelight is a wonderful idea; citronella candles will help repel insects. Place votive candles in decorative holders and scatter them about the porch or patio.

BELOW: An enclosed porch becomes a nature-inspired haven when furnished with a beautiful wicker chaise longue and garden accessories. Lattice panels help filter sunlight, create privacy, and contribute architectural design. The sisal matting on the floor is in keeping with a casual outdoor theme. A striking folding screen and a tablescape of dried flowers, baskets, and terra-cotta pots become stunning attractions.

OPPOSITE: A high-rise terrace has been transformed into a spectacular garden retreat, thanks to brick flooring, white wooden fencing, and numerous terra-cotta pots filled with colorful blooms. An elevated platform, complete with a chaise longue, becomes a secluded garden bower with the addition of a fabric canopy and curtains.

ABOVE: A glass-enclosed sunroom is the ideal way to bring the outdoors inside for year-round pleasure and enjoyment. This elegant space is furnished with lovely white wicker, accessorized with floral cushions and assorted throw pillows. Several potted plants and a magnificent hanging fern pay tribute to the garden theme, which is accentuated by the stately tree beyond the French doors. Lovely light fixtures—a torchère and a reproduction chandelier—allow the room to be enjoyed both day and night.

Furnishings

Furnishing outdoor spaces for the traditional home is a matter of taste and comfort. Furniture should be casual and carefree, but it can still impart style. Ideally, the porch or patio will include a selection of furnishings to meet your every need for seating, lounging, and alfresco meals or snacks. Cedar or redwood furniture with crisp, clean lines is quite attractive and can be stained or allowed to weather to a lovely silvery gray. Hammocks and Adirondack chairs have long been used in outdoor spaces and are the ultimate in comfort and relaxing style.

Wicker furniture is a natural on the porch, and you can scout antiques shops, shows, and auctions for authentic pieces or buy quality reproductions. Old wicker furnishings were actually crafted from reed, willow, cane, or rattan and constructed with hardwood frames. During the early twentieth century, paper-fiber wicker was introduced, and furnishings made of this are better suited to the indoors. When buying vintage wicker, check to make sure that the piece is structurally sound, and look closely for damage such as missing bits of fiber. Restoring wicker furniture can be costly and is best left to the expertise of a professional.

Since wicker furnishings were widely popular during and after the Victorian age, numerous items were created for home and outdoor use. For the porch, you may want to consider a selection of comfy rockers and chairs, a table or two, and perhaps a settee or sofa.

Accessorize seating with thick cotton-covered cushions and toss pillows. Fabric with a casual stripe or a floral pattern will complement wicker nicely.

Decorative accessories in an extended outdoor living area should have an outdoor theme. Classical urns, Victorian jardinieres, and countrified clay pots—all filled with blooms—go hand in hand with outdoor spaces. Larger wooden or wire plant stands will accommodate an entire collection of flowers or plants. And there is always the window box, which has long been favored as a mode of container gardening that adds instant color and charm to a home's façade. Also, consider hanging plants housed in wire containers, which provide a riot of color when scattered around the porch or hung from deck railings.

⬥⬥⬥

OPPOSITE: Pale yellow walls and a white tile floor create a pleasing backdrop for casual furnishings in this cheerful sunroom. The rugged texture of the wicker sofa contrasts nicely with the airy black metal chairs and table. Colorful pillows, fresh flowers, and a metal wall rack that holds small plants convey an outdoor theme. The French doors are left bare to enjoy the garden view.

RIGHT: Simplicity can be lovely, especially in a natural setting. This dark green garden bench is an inviting spot to relax and take a break from tending flowers and plants. Sculpted and potted shrubs in terra-cotta pots and a graceful statue give this serene retreat a traditional ambience. Even the gardener's tools—watering can, clippers, and gloves—become decorative elements that add color and style.

Gardens, Conservatories, and Sunrooms

Moving off the porch and out into the garden, a quiet spot with a wooden bench or comfortable wooden chair may serve as a natural oasis. Expanding upon this idea, some homeowners opt for a lovely gazebo, once referred to as a summerhouse, in a secluded spot by shade trees or a favorite garden. During the late 1800s, the gazebo was often patterned after a Japanese teahouse, and this exotic air was in keeping with the fascination for anything of Oriental design. Common designs today, however, reflect a more rustic or Victorian look. Gazebos are usually constructed with built-in seating in the form of benches, and they can be used for anything from simple relaxation to evening suppers and lawn parties.

For the homeowner or apartment dweller who doesn't have the luxury of a porch or patio, inside spaces can be made to feel like outdoor havens. A sunroom, conservatory, or even something as basic as a back-door breezeway can be used to full advantage in warm weather.

Conservatories have been popular in Great Britain for centuries, and they achieved popularity in North America during the 1800s. These spaces, enclosed by glass windows, are ideal for everything from gardening to entertaining. The conservatory features a cool tile, brick, or slate floor and is best outfitted with casual furnishings that hint at total relaxation. Filled with lush greenery and potted flowers as well as decorative cushions on chairs, chaise longues, and ottomans, the conservatory can be the most cherished spot in the house.

A sunroom can be an enclosed patio or a room with a sunny exposure that sports a wall of windows. Relaxed furnishings will work best in this area, and while wicker is a wonderful choice, you may prefer a casual blend of wooden and upholstered pieces to create a different look. Play up the garden or outdoor theme with sun-filtering shades at the windows, and surround the setting with potted plants and flowers.

Last but not least, since outdoor spaces have close ties to flowers and gardening, you may want to set aside a corner in a breezeway or on the patio for gardening tools. Unless you have the luxury of a potting shed, an old worktable or cupboard can do nicely and can actually look quite attractive and decorative. For example, you can create an eye-catching tablescape with clay pots, ceramic containers, galvanized pails for fresh flowers, a vintage watering can, and garden tools. Hang an antique botanical print above this workstation for inspiration and decoration. Even if gardening isn't your passion, be sure to allow time to savor the moments spent with family and friends on the traditional front porch or patio.

❧❧❧

RIGHT: Reminiscent of those architectural gems—the widow's walk or the Victorian turret—this elevated hideaway was designed to savor the view. A rocking chair, a telescope, favorite books, and flowers are all that's needed in the way of simple pleasures. As dusk approaches, the wall sconces and wrought-iron chandelier provide soft lighting.
OPPOSITE: A formal garden is transformed into a secluded getaway with the addition of a latticed bower with a distinct Japanese roof. The lattice panels are covered with honeysuckle vines, which create a lush, fragrant privacy screen. Elaborate wrought-iron chairs, recalling nineteenth century designs, provide elegant garden seating.

✦

OPPOSITE: This spacious sunroom combines solid comfort with elegant beauty. Resilient flooring with a geometric design is an easy-care treatment for a casual space. Windows are dressed with dark green Roman shades that give the room a tailored look. Furnishings—in a blend of rattan and handsome wood—are joined by a plump sofa covered with cushions in a cheerful mix of stripes and a floral print.

ABOVE: This warm and inviting sunroom features a gleaming plank floor and rustic wooden furnishings that give the space a relaxed country air. The rugged good looks of the wood are juxtaposed with the elegant decanter and stemware and the classic appeal of a lovely urn-shaped container filled with flowers.

ABOVE: This beautiful sunroom features windows with classic architectural flair. Casual bamboo furnishings with plump cushions are the ideal choice for an indoor garden room. Lush ferns and other greenery make this an outdoor oasis in a winter wonderland.

OPPOSITE: The beauty of the small formal garden can be enjoyed from the garden bench when weather allows, or from the handsome conservatory when the climate is less inviting. The venerable conservatory, the ultimate garden room, was long favored in England and became popular in North America during the 1800s. This striking example gives architectural flair to the home and creates welcome additional living space.

SOURCES

Accessories for the Home

By Good Hands
P.O. Box 4104
Portsmouth, NH 03801
(603) 547-2011
Specializes in decorative accessories for the colonial-period room. Call or write for information on available portfolio.

Crate & Barrel
725 Landwehr Road
Northbrook, IL 60065
(800) 606-6387
Call for store locations.

Raymond Enkeboll Designs
16506 Avalon Boulevard
Carson, CA 90746
(310) 532-1400
Specializes in architectural wood carvings. Call for a free brochure.

Renovator's
P.O. Box 2515
Conway, NH 03818
(800) 659-0203
Specializes in bath and lighting fixtures and decorative items for the home. Call for catalog.

Royal Design Studio
386 East H Street
Suite 209-188
Chula Vista, CA 91910
(800) 747-9767
Specializes in stencils for decorative paintwork.

Yowler & Shepps
3529 Main Street
Conestoga, PA 17516
(717) 872-2820
Specializes in stencils for decorative paintwork. Call for catalog.

Furniture for the Home

Arthur Brett & Sons (USA) Ltd.
330 North Hamilton Street
High Point, NC 27260
Specializes in reproduction English furniture with design trade showrooms across the country. Write for a free brochure.

Baker Furniture
P.O. Box 1887
Grand Rapids, MI 49501
(800) 592-2537
Call for list of retailers.

Bartley Collection Ltd.
65 Engerman Avenue
Denton, MD 21629
(800) 787-2800
Specializes in antique reproduction furniture kits including Queen Anne, Chippendale, Federal, and Shaker styles.

British Khaki Furniture
62 Greene Street
New York, NY 10012
(212) 343-2299

Cohasset Colonials
10 Churchill Road
Hingham, MA 02043
(800) 288-2389
Specializes in museum-quality reproductions available assembled, either finished or unfinished, and as kits.

Drexel Heritage Furniture
101 North Main Street
Drexel, NC 28619
(704) 433-3000

Harden Furniture
8550 Mill Pond Way
McConnellsville, NY 13401
(315) 245-1000
Write for a free color brochure.

Magnolia Hall
726 Andover Drive
Atlanta, GA 30327
(404) 351-1910
Specializes in Victorian reproduction furniture. Call for catalog.

L. & J.G. Stickley Company
P.O. Box 480
Manlius, NY 13104
(315) 682-5500
Specializes in Arts and Crafts–style oak and cherry furniture. Call for catalog.

Thomasville
401 East Main Street
Thomasville, NC 27361
(800) 225-0265

Yield House
P.O. Box 2525
Conway, NH 03818
(800) 659-0206
Specializes in Shaker- and country-style furnishings. Call for catalog.

Furniture for Outdoor Spaces

Currey & Company
200 Ottley Drive
Atlanta, GA 30324
(404) 885-1444
Specializes in reproduction bamboo furnishings.

Lloyd/Flanders
P.O. Box 550
Menominee, MI 49858
(888) CASUAL-2
Specializes in reproduction and contemporary wicker furnishings suitable for outdoors. Call for dealer locations.

Smith & Hawken
117 East Strawberry Drive
Mill Valley, CA 94941
(800) 776-3336
Specializes in garden furniture and other items available via mail order. Call for catalog.

Kitchen Cabinetry for the Home

Crownpoint Cabinetry
153 Charlestown Road
P.O. Box 1560
Claremont, NH 03743
(800) 999-4994

Plain & Fancy Custom Cabinetry
P.O. Box 519
Schaefferstown, PA 17088
(800) 447-9006
Call for dealer locations.

Lighting for the Home

Graham's Lighting
550 South Cooper
Memphis, TN 38104
(800) 362-8099
Specializes in reproduction chandeliers.

Rejuvenation Lamp & Fixture Co.
1100 S.E. Grand Avenue
Portland, OR 97214
(503) 231-1900
Specializes in authentic reproduction chandeliers, sconces, porch lights, and Arts and Crafts, Victorian, and neoclassical styles.

Sedgefield
216 Woodbine Street
High Point, NC 27260
(910) 882-0196

Schonbek Worldwide Lighting Inc.
61 Industrial Boulevard
Plattsburgh, NY 12901
(800) 836-1892
Specializes in crystal chandeliers.

Paint for Furnishings and the Home

Cohasset Colonials
10 Churchill Road
Hingham, MA 02043
(800) 288-2389
Specializes in reproduction paints with the look of old milk paints for furniture, walls, and woodwork.

Dutch Boy Paints
101 Prospect Avenue
Cleveland, OH 44115
(800) 828-5669

Pratt & Lambert Paints
P.O. Box 22
Buffalo, NY 14240
(800) 289-7728

Sherwin Williams Co.
101 Prospect Avenue
Cleveland, OH 44115
(800) 4-SHERWIN

Rugs and Carpeting for the Home

Clair Murray
P.O. Box 390
Ascutney, VT 05030
(800) 252-4733
Specializes in hand-hooked rugs, quilts, and kits. Call for catalog.

Couristan
2 Executive Drive
Fort Lee, NJ 07024
(800) WE-LUV-RUGS

J.R. Burrows & Co.
P.O. Box 522
Rockland, MA 02370
(617) 982-1812
Specializes in reproduction nineteenth-century rugs and carpets and offers Victorian wallpapers, fabrics, and lace curtains.

Karastan Carpets
P.O. Box 12070
Calhoun, GA 30703
(800) 234-1120

Mohawk Carpets
P.O. Box 12069
Calhoun, GA 30703
(800) 241-4494

Wall Coverings and Fabrics for the Home

Bradbury & Bradbury
P.O. Box 155
Benicia, CA 94510
(707) 746-1900
Specializes in nineteenth-century reproduction wallpapers. Call for catalog.

Mt. Diablo Handprints Inc.
P.O. Box 726
Benecia, CA 94510
(707) 745-3388
Specializes in reproduction historical wallpapers. Call for catalog.

Arthur Sanderson and Sons, Ltd.
979 Third Avenue
New York, NY 10022
(800) 533-8229

Thibaut
480 Frelinghuysen Avenue
Newark, NJ 07114
(800) 223-0704
Call for availability in your area.

Window Curtains for the Home

Country Curtains
The Red Lion Inn
Stockbridge, MA 01262
(800) 876-6123
Specializes in a wide variety of curtains appropriate for the traditional home. Call for catalog.

Linen & Lace
4 Lafayette Street
Washington, MO 63090
(314) 239-6499
Specializes in imported Scottish lace curtains. Call for catalog.

INDEX